Polymer Clay
and Mixed Media
together at last

Creative Publishing international

First published in the United States of America by
Creative Publishing international, Inc., a member of
Quayside Publishing Group
400 First Avenue North
Suite 300
Minneapolis, MN 55401
1-800-328-3895
www.creativepub.com

ISBN-13: 978-1-58923-433-8
ISBN-10: 1-58923-433-2

10 9 8 7 6 5 4 3 2

Library of Congress Cataloging-in-Publication Data
Friesen, Christi.
  Polymer clay and mixed media, together at last : incorporating craft materials and found objects in clay figures / by Christi Friesen.
     p. cm.
  Includes bibliographical references and index.
  ISBN 978-1-58923-433-8 (alk. paper)
  1. Polymer clay craft. 2. Handicraft. I. Title.

TT297.F755 2008
745.5--dc22

                                                        2008023561

Cover and Book Design: doublemranch.com
Page Layout: doublemranch.com
Illustrations: Christi Friesen
Photographs: Christi Friesen
Copy Editor: Sarah Erdreich
Proofreader: Iris Bass

Printed in Singapore

Polymer Clay

and Mixed Media

together at last

Incorporating craft materials and
found objects in clay figures

Christi Friesen

Creative Publishing
international

Contents

Introduction

Polymer clay and mixed media together at last!

Polymer clay is an amazing medium—colorful, light-weight, durable, and so easy to use. You just can't put the stuff down once you start to play with it. Now add mixed media—which are all the other fun things in the world of arts and crafts, such as papers, paints, metals, glass, beads, fibers—and you can see this is going to be a full-blown addiction. The good kind, of course, like chocolate.

This book is all about combining polymer clay with other materials. Other craft materials and art media have been used with polymer clay for as long as the clay has been available, but this book sets out to open new windows of possibility. New ways to create.

Oh, and have lots and lots of fun.

Overview

Using Polymer Clay with Mixed Media

Whether you've created with polymer clay and mixed media for ages or never touched the stuff, you may have some questions: Which clays should you use? What tools should you have? What other materials can safely be used with polymer clay? What's that shiny powder for? Should you eat milk chocolate or dark chocolate to stimulate creativity? (Ok, maybe not that last one.) Here are the answers to most of your questions.

Clay Basics

I always prefer to play (don't you?), but sometimes you have to know the particulars of the game first in order to have more fun playing. So, if you skip this overview part and head right to the projects, I won't blame you a bit (I do it all the time myself). Just know the information is right here if you need it! Oh, and there's more at the end of the book, too—just like in math class when you can flip to the back for the answers to check your work.

POLYMER CLAYS

Polymer clay has been around for decades. There are several major brands and all are very similar in composition and in how they are used. Check out the descriptions of the brands on page 153. New clays and re-formulations of existing clay brands are constantly becoming available, so browse online or in your local craft stores to see what's new!

Polymer clay brands can usually be mixed together with no ill effects, at least for all these sculpting projects. So if your clays get jumbled together, no worries! Just condition them thoroughly together, and use with confidence.

For the projects in this book, I have used mostly Premo! clays. They're my personal favorite. All the color recipes will be based on Premo! colors. If you use a different brand, just substitute a similar color—it should work out just fine!

◀ Yay! Clay! Polymer clays come in 2 oz. (56.7 g) packages and 1 lb. (0.45 kg) blocks, as well as in special combination packages.

STORAGE

Polymer clay does not air dry. It needs heat to set at a specific temperature to cure fully. You should always store polymer clays in a cool place, away from sunlight (and the possible resulting rise in temperature). Once the clay is unwrapped from the plastic packaging, leaving it on a porous surface (like wood or paper) is not a good idea. The components of the polymer clay mix that make it soft and pliable will leach out, eventually making the clay crumbly and dry. It's not too great for the surface of the lovely antique credenza that you left the clay on, either. So, after you're done with your project for the day, the best way to store your clay is in plastic bags (I'm partial to the zippered ones) or between sheets of waxed paper. You can do the same with an unfinished creation—set it inside a plastic bag or cover the top and bottom with waxed paper. Some plastic containers react with polymer clay and the two form a kind of inseparable bond, so stick with the bags or wax paper. Of course, you can stick the bags in a plastic container. And the containers in a box and the whole pile of clays and tools and books and beads and boxes and other goodies in one of those big rolling cart thingies and join the ranks of the true polymer addicts! (Just attend a polymer clay guild* and you'll see what I mean.)

▲ Polymer clays all zipped up and waiting for when you're ready to play again.

*Polymer clay guild? What's that?
(See Resources in the back of the book for more information!)

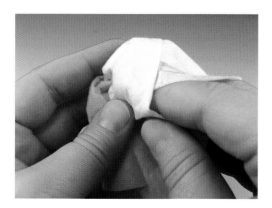

▲ Baby wipes—not just for bottoms anymore!

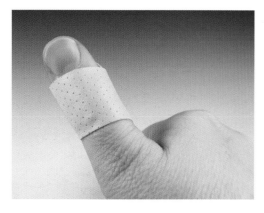

▲ If you do get poked or cut, use this. Blood never looks good on a finished project (the pretty red gets too brown once it's baked).

SAFETY

Polymer clays are safe and nontoxic. They have been tested to be so by the ACMI (Arts & Crafts Materials Institute). Of course, you always have to use common sense—you wouldn't want to make a habit of eating polymer clay, or anything silly like that. Here are a few simple guidelines to follow that will help make using polymer clay fun and safe:

1. Wash your hands after using polymer clays.
2. Don't poke, jab, or cut yourself with the tools.
3. Use ventilation when baking polymer clays.

That about covers it.

Well, a few more details are probably in order. First, washing your hands to remove polymer clay residue is just smart. The skin on your hands is one big permeative surface, so residue left on it after working with your clay will be somewhat absorbed into your body. It's just smart to try to minimize that as much as possible. Polymer clay doesn't come off easily with plain ol' soap and water, so use gritty soap, or even baby oil or lotions. After that, soap and water will finish the job. It's very handy to have a container of baby wipes to remove clay residue while you work. You'll especially need them on warm or humid days, or if you have hot li'l hands! The warmth makes some clays more than others stick to your skin so wiping frequently while you're working keeps the buildup down.

Second: no cutting, jabbing, or poking. This is pretty self-explanatory. With polymer clay projects, you'll use needle tools and cutting blades and other potentially stabby objects. And if you're creating these projects with children, keep an eye on them—the littlest fingers always seem to find the sharpest tools. It's a kid thing.

Finally, use ventilation when baking. You know, there's enough to say about baking that it deserves its own subject heading (next page).

OK, so those are some safety tips for working with polymer clay. How about some overall safety tips concerning the mixed media objects that will also be a part of these projects? Sure, why not!

Common sense applies to most things. Some projects call for glass or metal embellishments—be careful with sharp edges. Wear safety goggles if you're cutting glass or metal or anything liable to fly up and get in your eyes. Some projects call for adding varnishes or resin-like materials—use gloves and cover your work surface if you're worried about stains. Use ventilation! You know, all the usual precautions. If in doubt, read the instructions. Do what you would make your children do if they were working with the materials.

BAKING

Baking is the most important element of success in creating with polymer clay. You can create the most marvelous thing in the known universe, but if it scorches, melts, or breaks because it's undercooked, what's the point?

Polymer clay needs to be baked in a regular oven for it to become the hardened, durable product we know and love. While it is baking, the clay does produce fumes, which some people are sensitive to. And, with fumes of any kind, it is always a good idea to use adequate ventilation—the oven's overhead fan, or an open window. Over time, the slight residue from the clay builds up in your oven, so the fumes may become stronger. Also, as the oven reheats to cook your food, that reheated residue can get into your food. That's not good. So, if you use the same oven for clay as you do for food baking, clean your oven frequently! Since I don't like cleaning, I have a separate little oven just for polymer clay. Many polymer clayers do, too, for obvious reasons. Who wants to clean their ovens that much? (Or for that matter, who wants to bake food that much? Let's all just go out to a restaurant for dinner instead!)

You'll probably find that a toaster oven or convection oven that is solely used for baking polymer clay will make your life easier. Electric or gas ovens are fine. Microwave ovens are not, since controlling the temperature is very important. There is no specific brand of oven that is overwhelmingly better than any other for baking clay. Many clayers have found that cheap toaster ovens often have problems with temperature consistency (they go from "lukewarm" to "volcano" in seconds), so you should probably avoid those "bargains." But a good oven isn't necessarily expensive—most department stores and kitchen stores usually carry a nice, medium-size oven at a good price.

If polymer clay is baked above its recommended temperature, it will darken and scorch. That means your project will look burnt and there will be crying or cursing (depending on your personality and how you react to disappointment). If the temperature gets too high, it will burn, blister, and smoke—and smoke is definitely something you don't want inside your house! So, make sure the temperature <u>inside</u> your oven is correct by using a dependable oven thermometer. Many ovens come from the store with a gremlin preinstalled at the factory whose job it is to make your oven's temperature a mystery. (I'm kidding, probably.) Place the oven thermometer on the pan that you will bake on and put the pan in the center of the oven. Test-bake your oven first to see where you need to set the oven's dial for the interior temperature to be correct. Sometimes the knob can be 50°F

▲ A gremlin comes optional with some oven models.

▲ A good oven thermometer is a must-have!

Hey! No poking!

(10°C) or more off calibration! Once you figure out where to set the dial, it's a good idea to mark the knob with a marker or tape—but keep that thermometer inside, just in case the gremlin gets up to his tricks! (And as ovens get older, sometimes the temperature calibration changes as well.)

Polymer clays usually bake at 265°–275°F (130°–135°C). A temperature that's too low will leave the clay seemingly done but actually brittle and easily chipped and broken. If the temperature is too high, it's that whole scorching, smoking, meltdown thing again. Check the packaging of your clay to see exactly what the manufacturer recommends. If your clays are a mystery mix and you don't remember which brands they are anymore, you can confidently bake at 265°–275°F (130°–135°C).

At the time of this writing, several of the major brands are reformulating their clays to have lower baking temperatures. Of course this will affect your cooking specifics, especially if they get mixed in with higher-baking brands. So, please check the clay's printed instructions, and visit the company's website for the most up-to-date information on baking temperatures.

Finally, the length of time you bake your piece for is determined by the overall thickness of the piece. The clay manufacturers usually recommend about 20 minutes for every ¼" (6 mm) of thickness at the thickest part of the piece. The clay has to get to the correct temperature all the way through the piece for the polymer clay to be properly cured. Polymer clay has a "give" to it when cooked properly—it will bend, not break. Undercooked clays will crack and break—so don't rush the baking process!

For all the projects in this book, you can expect the pieces to be in the oven for anywhere from 30 minutes to an hour. If in doubt, go for 45 minutes and you'll be fine!

Oh, and by the way, when your clay is all cooked but still hot, it will be rubbery, not hard! It hardens as it cools, so just leave it alone (it's still fragile at this stage). No poking, yanking, or dropping!

Another thing to know about baking polymer clay: you can bake for shorter periods of time as a way of setting details, then add more fresh clay details and bake again. There's no limit to how many times in one project you do this. Liquid clay applied to the baked clay where you want to attach the fresh clay will make this work beautifully. Once you are all done with the short bakes, the final baking will be for the full time (as if you hadn't done the short bakes at all). One word of caution, clay does have a tendency to darken a little as it bakes, and multiple bakings may cause your piece to darken even more.

Tools and Supplies

The fun thing about polymer clay is that you really don't need to spend much money on tools and supplies to get started. Of course, you <u>can</u> spend all kinds of money on tools if you want to—that's always fun, but you don't have to (unlike some arts or crafts for which expensive tools, equipment, and training are a necessity). Besides the clay, all you really need are some fingers (at least five will work, ten are better), and a simple tool or two to poke and prod the clay into shape. Here are some of the tools you probably should have, and some tools that are just fun to have.

Many of these tools and supplies are not specifically designed for working with clay, so you won't necessarily find them in the same aisle as the clay at the craft store. Some items you may already have hiding in drawers around your home. I can think of one in particular that you'll find in a kitchen supply store, if you don't already have one. (Hint: look in the Italian cooking section.)

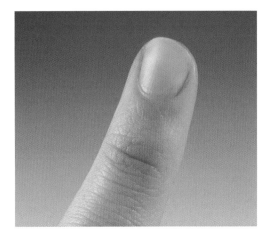

▲ Fingers! The best tool for polymer clay, ever!

▲ Needle tools, dowel tools, and other pokey tools

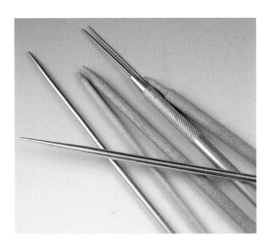

▲ Paint brushes to apply patina, color wash, and clear coating; sponges

▲ Wire cutters

▲ Paper to work on and to cook on. This keeps your piece from sticking to the work surface, and from getting shiny by contact with the metal pan when it's being baked. Use a heavier paper, like card stock or index cards.

▲ Embossing tools and other ball-ended tools

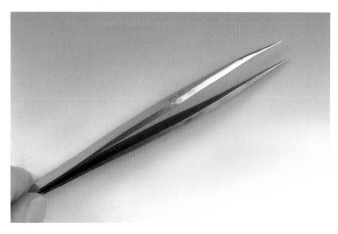

▲ Needle-nose tweezers (long nose and no teeth, just like uncle Harold!)

▲ Texture tools—anything that you can press into the clay to impress an interesting image or pattern

▼ Wire: thin (28-gauge) to attach beads to the clay; medium (22-gauge, 20-gauge, and 18-gauge) for support, hanging loops, and pendant loops; and heavy (16-gauge and higher) for armatures

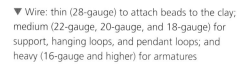

▼ Pliers—chain nose, round nose, and crimping

▲ Things that cut and slice—craft knives, cutting blades, and good ol' dependable scissors

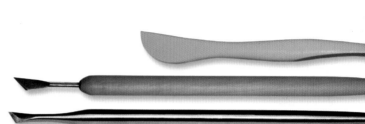

▲ My favorite tools!!! The "Gotta Have It" tool and the "Can't Live Without It" tool (two sizes). See Resources, page 154.

▲ Glues and adhesives

▲ Wooden, plastic, and metal sculpting tools (and things that aren't sculpting tools, but work great as such—like dental tools)

▼ Pasta machine, roller (optional—works if you don't have a pasta machine or to flatten the clay before rolling through the pasta machine)

▼ Acrylic paint for patinas and color washes

Getting Ready

OK, so you've got your tools in front of you, and your packages of clays—now what? Before we can leap right into the projects, let's chat about conditioning the clay and mixing colors.

CONDITIONING

Conditioning your clay is necessary before you do anything else. The clay needs to be warmed up. Break off a small bit of clay and roll it in your hands to warm it. (Or you can use a roller if you want to.) Fold and reroll that snake of clay until it bends easily when you fold it. Of course, a pasta machine makes this process faster and it's a lot easier on the hands. Simply roll and flatten the clay, then set the pasta machine to the widest setting and run the clay through. Fold the clay sheet and run it through again and again until it is soft and pliable. Usually six to a dozen times through will do it.

To minimize air bubbles, put the clay in fold-first. But don't stress about air bubbles for the projects in this book—sculpture is very forgiving—just poke the bubble, smooth it, and put a little clay dot or curl to cover any problem areas.

One last bit about conditioning—if you have clay that's crumbly, roll it and soften it in your hands as much as you can (often that's all it needs), but if it's still being naughty, you can add a drop or two of clay softener or liquid clay. Knead it in and continue conditioning.

MIXING AND COLOR BLENDS

Polymer clay has color, baby! That's probably its most attractive feature, actually. The ability to create in color is irresistible. As a colored medium, it is unique—the color will hold its integrity when pieced together with different colors, with no bleeding. But different colors can be mixed together to make stripes, swirls, blushes, and entirely new colors. Now that's magical!

Here are ways that polymer colors can be mixed—try 'em all!

Fully blended: Take two or more colors of clay and smoosh them together, then run through the pasta machine as many times as needed to create a completely new color with no streaks or variations.

Partially blended: Do the same as fully blended, but STOP blending while some streaks and variations are still visible. Very marbley.

Custom blends: Add specific bits of clay, or inclusions such as powders to the clay to create a customized look.

Multicolor twist

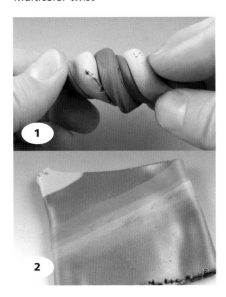

Adding cane slices

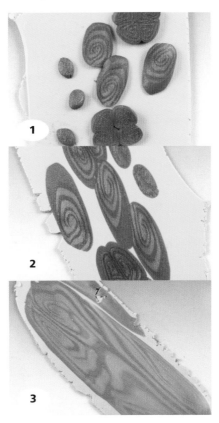

Adding powders

1. Use several colors of clay and roll each into a little log, press the logs together, and twist.

2. Run through the pasta machine.

3. Repeat steps 1 and 2 until a nice blend is achieved.

1. Cut off thin slices of cane (we'll get to canes in a minute), and lay them on the surface of a sheet of clay.

2. Run through the pasta machine to distort the pattern.

3. If you want, you can fold the clay with the most interesting part of the pattern showing and run through the pasta machine once more.

1. Add powders to the center of the sheet of clay and fold the clay around it, wrapping it inside.

2. Run this through the pasta machine repeatedly until the powder is evenly distributed (this works best with light-colored or translucent clays).

Skinner blend

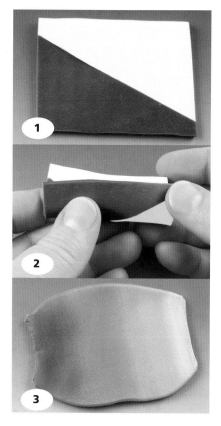

Lookit blend

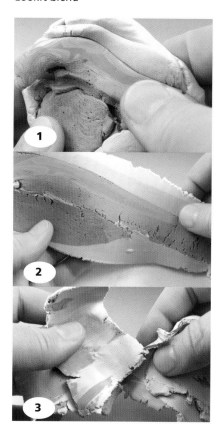

This blend is a brilliant way of making an even gradation from one color to another.

1. Roll out two sheets of clay, cut each into a rectangle, slice each diagonally, and then line 'em up.

2. Fold and run through the pasta machine, repeat—always folding and running through in the same direction.

3. Tah dah! a perfect gradation of color!

OK, this is one I made up, but it's fun and you'll like it! It's based on the same principle as the Skinner blend, only loose and sloppy.

1. Smash several colors of clay together.

2. Run them through the pasta machine to flatten.

3. Rip the sheet and reposition for maximum color concentration.

4. Run it through, lookit both sides, and then fold it up so the coolest stuff is in the front.

5. The blend is starting, but it's too loud. Run it through again, lookit both sides, and fold it up and through the pasta machine again. Repeat until you get to say …

6. … LOOKIT! what a cool blend! I should use it for a sky or oceany thing!

CANES

While we're talking about color, there's one more way to combine polymer clay to take advantage of its wonderful color properties—make canes. Canes are a combination of clay pieces that form a pattern. Caning is an art form in itself, and was developed early in the history of polymer clay creations to mimic the glass "millefiori" techniques. Many people feel polymer clay is actually a much better medium for this craft than glass is. Many polymer books are devoted to canes, so if you are interested, you'll have lots of possibilities. We'll use the concept in this book, but they will be simple and small (many canes use pounds and pounds of clay to create). But big or small, the principles are the same. Here's what you need to know to get by for the projects in this book.

When making a cane, make sure you press all the pieces together firmly to eliminate gaps and air bubbles.

All canes are "reduced" to make them smaller and more compact. Reducing can be done in a number of ways, but the goal is to make the piece smaller with as little distortion as possible. So pull and press instead of rolling to lengthen and narrow the cane.

Canes are created so that their cross sections will be visible. Cut these sections with a very sharp cutting blade only, otherwise the cut will mush, ruining the design.

Store canes in waxed paper or plastic wrap, so that they don't touch any other clay.

Here's the world's simplest cane (a jelly roll) to get the feel of it!

1. Roll out two sheets of clay, lay one on top of the other and trim into a rectangle, pinch one end flatter (this will help it roll up better).
2. Roll it up firmly.
3. Reduce it to a quarter of its diameter, by pulling and pressing along the roll.
4. Cut slices as needed.

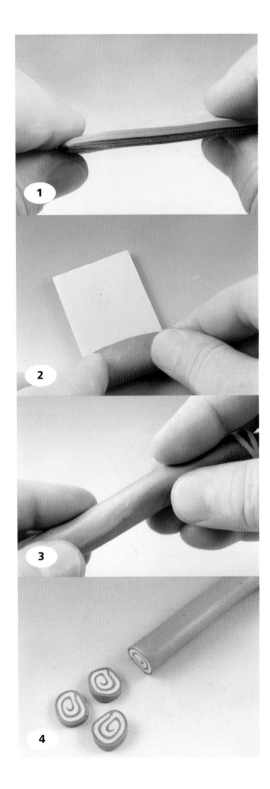

▲ Fibers, fabric, and paper

▲ Beads

▲ Natural materials

Adding Mixed Media

WHAT IS MIXED MEDIA ANYWAY?

The term "mixed media" is used to describe an art piece that has been created with multiple types of materials (media)—a mixture. Makes sense, huh? It has also come to be a rather generic term to apply to the large range of materials available to use in creating (as opposed to specific media like ceramic, glass, or watercolor, for example).

Since we'll be using polymer clay as our main medium and combining it with other mixed media (together at last, remember?)—which media can be used? And how?

Here's my theory—anytime something can be used with and added to the clay while the clay is fresh and uncured, it will be more permanent and nicer looking than something added on afterward. I'm not a big glue person—if I can attach it with minimal gluing, I'm happier. I think it prevents the mess that glue sometimes leaves, and makes the bond more permanent if it's baked into the clay. Having said that, there are times when glue is the best option! But let's see what we can do without it, shall we?

Any item that can handle being in the oven at 275°F (130°C) for 45 minutes to an hour without burning, melting, scorching, or splitting works great when added to the clay. This includes all metals (as well as metal leaf and foil), glass and mirror (glass beads as well, of course), stones, pearls, crystal, minerals, fossils, ceramics of all types, natural furs, feathers, wool, fiber, cloth, fabric and laces, enameled metals, shells, sand, and rock. Some things like wood and other dried seeds and plant materials will work, some will not. You can't always depend on wood to be cured properly, it may warp or crack, or sap bubbles might rise to the surface (and that's not good). Some resins work, others melt. Plastic usually melts, but some man-made fibers, such as polyester, are fine. If in doubt, place a bit of the craft material on a piece of foil and pop it in the oven at 275°F (130°C) and see what happens. (Use good ventilation, of course, in case it's a melter!)

A few materials, like EnviroTex (a clear resinlike product) are added afterward to the baked clay, since they can't handle the heat.

Here are some mixed media that we'll be using in the projects. Look in Resources (page 154) for information on where to find these items.

Fibers, Fabric, and Papers: Any natural fiber like wool, hemp, cotton, or silk will work, and most polyesters will, too. If in doubt, just put a snippet in the oven and see what happens. Any paper will work well in the oven as long as it doesn't touch the heating elements, of course.

Beads: This is my favorite medium to add to clay! Use natural pearls, glass beads of all kinds from seed beads to lampwork beads, gemstones and semiprecious stones, crystals, ceramic, and metal. Avoid plastic and resin beads, they melt. Glass pearls don't melt but their coatings usually scorch, so stick with real pearls.

Natural Materials: You have to be a little more careful in this category, as some things like wood and seeds tend to crack in the heat of the oven. But go crazy with shells, minerals, fossils, and feathers. Even straw, raffia, and fur work great.

Metal: Any metal object can be added to polymer clay. All metals work equally well—gold, silver, copper, steel, aluminum—so experiment with metal leafs and foils, chain, bead findings, wire, even metal mesh ribbon and electroplated items.

Glass: Like metal, all glass is good to go! So that means glass jars and bottles, mirrors, mini glass balls ("holeless beads"), dichroic glass cabochons, and more.

Found Objects: Use the other categories as a guide to what goes in this category—anything in metal, like screws, cutlery, money, bottlecaps, and that sort of thing will be terrific. Ceramic items such as plates and cabinet knobs are good. Natural items like paintbrush bristles will find new life in a clay creation. This gives you an excuse to pick through the trash (if you're into that sort of thing!).

Craft Items: You'll have to experiment to see what works in this very large category. Obviously, paints, pencils, and powders will add to the surface decoration on clay. Other items can be used either before the piece is baked, like acrylic gel mediums, or afterward, such as Paverpol and EnviroTex Lite resin.

▲ Metal

▲ Glass

▲ Found objects

▲ Craft items

▲ Ooooh! That tickles!

▲ So, these plugs look natural, right? 'Cuz I've got a big date tonight.

▲ This floral focal bead is all fancied up with beaded embellishments—and all of them are wired in!

USING LIQUID CLAY

Each of the major brands of clay has a liquid version available. Some are clear and some are milky when baked; some are thick and some are watery. All of them are great. As we go through the projects, you'll see that liquid clay is used to add strength, to attach clay details, and to give fresh clay a place to grab when adding it to baked clay. This also makes it great for repairing any broken or flawed areas in a baked piece. Just trim away the problem area, add liquid clay, and attach a new piece to replace the flaw.

Liquid clay is also my favorite way of attaching porous fibers to clay. Using liquid clay to soak into ribbon, lace, cloth, yarn, or wool, then allowing it to bake and fuse with the clay, makes those media permanently attached to the project without gluing. Yay! We'll talk about that when it comes up in the projects.

Liquid clay is not glue. You can't use it to make nonporous materials like glass or pearls stay put. We've got other ways to do that.

ADDING BEADS TO POLYMER CLAY

Ok, here's my favorite of all the mixed media additions. You'll notice a LOT of bead embellishments in all the projects in this book. Polymer clay and beads belong together. It's destiny. I didn't invent this combo, of course, but I like to think I helped popularize it. If you haven't added beads to polymer clay, you've missed half the fun! But no worries, you'll get your fill in these projects, I promise.

Since we don't want to use glue afterward to add beads (messy and undependable, remember?), we need a little trick to help them stay put. I discovered that wiring those babies in works great! A 28-gauge craft wire (uncoated metal in gold or silver color, usually) is the best to use—not too stiff, not too thin, juuuuuust right. The idea is to create a little tail of wire that is embedded into the clay when the bead is pressed into position. The baked clay will harden around that wire and thus keep the bead safe and secure.

All the different ways to wire up beads in order to achieve different looks are in the Tips and Techniques section beginning on page 146. Sorry, but almost no exceptions to the "wire it in" method of bead embellishing. If you just press the bead into the clay, be ready for it to pop out later. Are you appropriately concerned so that you will always wire in beads? Good.

SURFACE TREATMENTS

There are a lot of things that can be added to the surface of polymer clay—both while the clay is fresh and after it's baked. Some things, such as screen-printing onto clay, we won't play with in these projects, but check out other books and you'll find more ideas to explore. That's the cool thing about art—it's big and multifaceted, and everyone adds to it. It's probably one of the most important and impressive things about being human—this ability to create! Nobody has the corner on that market, we all share.

OK, moving on from philosophy. Some of the best things to add to the surface of polymer clay are mica and embossing powders and metal leafs and foils. We'll play with them all.

Mica powders are shiny. Embossing powders are not. With mica powders, you'll want to use a light touch to add just the kiss of glimmer. There are times when you want to cover the surface completely, but most of the time less is more. Use a soft-haired round brush (such as a watercolor brush), dip it in the powder, tap the powder into the lid, and use just that small amount to dust the surface of fresh clay. It'll stick right on and bake in. It's mostly permanent, but I always recommend adding a clear coating after the piece is baked to seal it and protect it if the piece is going to be worn.

Embossing powders are also applied to the surface, and pressing them in with your hand or a tool is best. Some puff and some almost melt, and some have a "distressed" look, so experiment by adding some to a scrap piece of clay and baking to make sure you like it before you slather it all over your masterpiece!

Metal leaf and foil can be real metal or imitation. If you can afford it, use the real stuff, it's nicer. Leafs and foils are laid directly onto the surface of a sheet of clay, where they grab instantly. You can use them just like that, or you can run the sheet through the pasta machine to make the clay stretch and crack the metal (which doesn't stretch). This crackle effect can be varied by how much you stretch the clay by putting it through wider or narrower settings on the pasta machine. You can also use the cover paper from the leaf/foil on top of the metal when running it through the machine to protect the metal.

Once clay is baked, you can't easily add powders or foils, but the surface will take wonderfully to additions of paint and pencil. I usually avoid most pens and markers since they can bleed (sometimes immediately, sometimes over time). Acrylic can be painted on directly. So can oil paints—but they take a while to dry and the piece is vulnerable during the drying process.

▲ Dust a glimmer of mica powder onto your project using a soft brush.

▲ On the left is the metal foil in gold color, on the right is real 23-karat gold leaf. Since gold leaf is much more malleable, it does stretch somewhat with the clay to produce a much more delicate crackle effect.

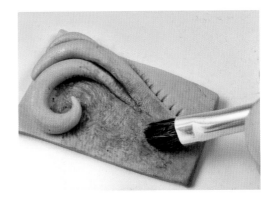

▲ Use a very thin coating of acrylic as a wash directly on the clay.

▲ If you add pencil to baked clay, use a pencil with a soft creamy lead, like these Prismacolors.

▲ A patina adds a little character to your project by enhancing all the creases, dimples, and lines.

▲ Brush on a clear coating to protect surface treatment.

BAKING TRICKS

When you're working with mixed media in clay, it's very helpful to have a few baking tricks up your sleeve (if you're wearing short sleeves, you may keep the tricks in your pocket). Remember that polymer clay can be baked multiple times. This really helps to set difficult items like ribbon or wool. Usually these little "prebakes" or "partial bakes" should be for about 20–25 minutes. You cannot add things to the partially baked clay that need to stick in (like beads with their wire tails). So do that first before baking. You can also use a heat gun to set liquid clay, so don't forget that handy little tool! Let the piece cool completely before continuing to work.

Once you've completed the piece, no matter how many times you've prebaked, you still have to do a full, complete baking of the finished piece (the usual 45 minutes to an hour, in most cases). Polymer clay has to reach that full temperature all the way to the core to cure properly, so lots of little bakes don't do the trick.

FINISHING TOUCHES

When your piece is completely finished and baked, then what? Well, sometimes, nothing! It's done. But if you're a nut, like me, you'll want to indulge in one or two more steps. First is adding a patina. This simply means using acrylic paint to enhance the look with an antiquing effect. This often eliminates the chalky look polymer clay can sometimes have when baked, and it enriches all the little detail lines you may have done during sculpting. A complete how-to is on page 150.

If the piece is going to be worn (a focal bead, pendant, or brooch), I recommend adding a clear coating to protect the powders, paints, and other surface treatments you may have added, as well as to give it that lovely finished gleam. Clear coatings—varnishes, glosses, and glazes—come in high and low luster (shiny and not-so-shiny). For most of the projects in this book, the look is organic, so the shine should be very minimal—use a matte or satin finish. If you're going for a glass or glazed look, use a high gloss. Several products work well with polymer clay. Check out the back of the book for more details on what to use and where to find it.

After the patina is dry (if you added one), apply the clear coat directly to the clay, covering any surface treatments. DO NOT coat over any of the beads or other mixed media embellishments. It just makes 'em mad.

Let all your finishing touches dry and then place the piece on a fresh piece of card stock paper and pop it into the oven one more time to set everything. Fifteen minutes at 200°F (95°C) will do the trick.

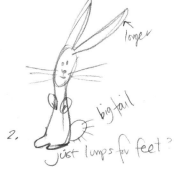

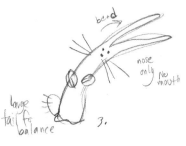

Doodling

Jumpstart Your Creativity!

Do you doodle? It's OK if you do—it's not like school or work, where you'll get in trouble for not paying attention. As an artist, doodling is a good thing. Think of it as a screen-saver function of your creativity programming. Your random doodlings will not always become your next fabulous masterpiece, but you'll almost always find a good idea or two among the scribbles!

Sketching out an idea is the more structured cousin of doodling—it's concentrated doodling to bring a vague concept into a more tangible idea. Sketching takes the ideas swirling around in your head and focuses them.

Here's an example of how the process can work. Let's say you doodled a bunny scribble that came out kinda cool. So now you want to make a clay bunny. OK, take that doodle and start sketching with the potential polymer clay version in mind. What if he's taller? Long whiskers? Maybe leaning over? Yeah, that looks good. Get rid of the feet and just make lumps. See how the sketching helps define the idea that the random doodle created?

Now your sketches are ready to guide your sculpting. Of course, the evolution of an idea doesn't stop—as you create with your clay, the process of creating will take over and often lead you in other directions. Clay does what it wants, and expects you to just follow. Sometimes the finished piece looks just like your sketch, sometimes it doesn't. It doesn't matter, it's all about the creating! Just have fun.

Oh, Grow Up!

Leaves, Flowers, and Growing Things

Glass-Centered Flower Beads, *page 44*

The variety of color, shape, and design in the plant world is pretty amazing. Throughout history, artists and craftsmen have portrayed plants and floral motifs in sculptures, mosaics, carvings, textiles…well, just everywhere. The method of portraying plant designs has often been stylized—not quite real, but certainly believable. "Stylizing" opens up big doors of possibility. To stylize a plant means to capture its look and feel and inner "plant," but not necessarily get hung up on being absolutely accurate.

Thistle Pin, *page 28*

Grapevine Mirror, *page 34*

For the projects in this section, you'll notice that the plants will be caricatures of themselves—simplified and stylized, so that the personality comes through. For example, the first project is a thistle pin. There are many varieties of thistles, in many colors (mostly in pinks and purples), but all thistles have two things in common—those spiky prickles and that tuft of hair on top! These elements, then, will be prominent in the project.

Ready? Let's grow!

Leaf and Flower Designs, *page 50*

Holly Berry Cluster Gift Tag, *page 40*

Look, Don't Touch
Thistle Pin

Size: 2½" (6.4 cm) tall

For this project you will need:

- all the usual sculpting tools
- cutting blade
- needle tool
- scissors
- 28-gauge wire
- pin back 1¼" or 1½" (3.18 or 3.8 cm)
- natural-bristle paintbrush
- liquid clay
- acrylic paint: Alizarin Crimson (or any other pink/purple), and blue
- mica powder (optional): pearl

So let's get started with this whole "stylized" thing by making a thistle pin, with that tuft of hair and prickly exterior really getting the attention.

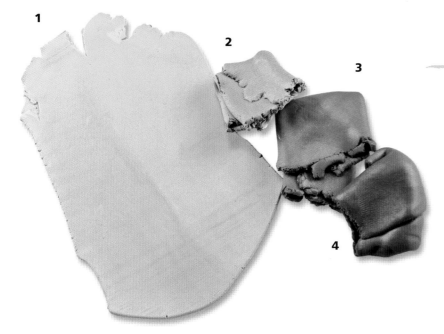

Clay Recipe

1. Background color: white + ecru + tiny amount each: gold, fuchsia, turquoise (amount: 1 oz.)
2. Light green: white + ecru + green pearl + tiny bit of gold (amount: 0.5 oz.)
3. Middle green: same mix as 1 + additional green pearl (amount: 0.5 oz.)
4. Dark green: same mix as 1 + sea green + burnt umber or additional green pearl + copper (amount: 0.5 oz.)

Clay mixing comes first. Start with the background color—a mix of white and ecru—just a bit more white than ecru is best. Next, add some turquoise and fuchsia and gold to create an earthy sort of pinkish lavender—not too bright, but with enough color to pick up on the pinkness in the thistle's top tuft (boy, try saying that ten times fast!). You only need a tiny smidgen of the colors to add to the white/ecru—a little color goes a long way. As you blend, remember to look it over for interesting streaks of color—stop mixing before it's all the way blended; a few hints of striations can look nice.

Next, mix the three variations of green. Start with an equal mix of white and ecru and blend thoroughly. Make a wad about the size of a walnut. Now add some green pearl (about half as much as the white/ecru) and a little smidgen of gold and mix thoroughly so that there are no streaks left. Divide this into thirds. One of these is your lightest green color. Set that aside. Now take the other two thirds and smash them back together (we'll split them up again later). Add more green pearl (and some more gold, too, if you want) and mix thoroughly until you have the middle green color. Now you can split that in half. Set one half aside. For the last green, use that last third section and mix in some see green and burnt umber, or more green pearl and a bit of copper clay—either combo will make a nice deeper green color.

▲ See? Prickles and spiky hair!

The spiky tufts at the top of the thistle are very important to the look. One of those inexpensive paintbrushes with natural, coarse bristles works perfectly!

1 Separate out a clump of the bristles that will become the tuft. Wrap a long strand of 28-gauge wire tightly around and around the bristle clump, then twist the ends of the wire firmly together (use pliers if your fingers can't do the trick). With wire cutters, snip off the excess to leave a tail of the twisted wire 1" or 2" (2.5 or 5 cm) in length.

2 Now squirt some liquid clay into the clump, close to the wire. Wipe off the excess with a bit of tissue, and bake it at 250°F (120°C) for about 10–15 minutes to set the liquid clay. This will make sure all the bristles are firmly attached so your thistle pin won't shed! (Nobody likes a shedding thistle pin.) Let it cool completely.

3 The best way to make those bristles pink is to paint them pink! Use acrylic paint, since it's permanent once it dries. My favorite is Alizarin Crimson, a delicious deep fuchsia color, just right for thistle thatch! Gloop out a little blob and moisten the tip of the wired bristle clump slightly, and dab it in the paint. Stroke the brush around in the paint, until the color is saturated, but not clumpy. The bristles should be delicately pink, not plastic-coated. Let it dry thoroughly.

OK, now cut the pink bristle clump off the paintbrush with scissors right below the wire wrap.

4 Time to turn that tuft into a flower's hairdo! Make a ball of the lightest green clay, about the size of a grape, and flatten it a bit with your fingers. Lay the bristle clump on top, with the wire-wrapped part just below the upper edge of the clay.

5 Now, fold the clay all around the bristle clump. Shape the clay into a ball around the bristles. Press the clay close against the bristles at the wire end, and keep it wider and more rounded at the bottom. As you shape the clay, smooth away any gaps, holes, or wrinkles until you have a nice rounded blob sprouting a tuft of pink hair. Yup, just like that.

6 Now pinch and pull the bottom, rounded end of the clay to start forming the stem. Do this by gently pinching out a little nub and elongating it. Take your time and keep moving the piece around in your hands to make it smooth and symmetrical. This won't be a full stem—there's not enough extra clay for that—it will just be the beginning of a stem.

7 To make the look even more believable, use a dowel tool or other sculpting tool to drag the top edge of the clay into the bristles.

Now add the rest of the stem—just smoosh a bit more of the lightest green clay onto the end of the nub and press and squeeze until it's attached and looking like it belongs. Elongate it so that you have a nice long stem—longer is better than shorter. You can always cut off the excess later.

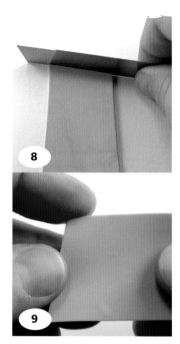

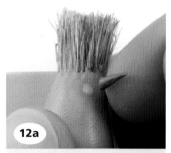

8

9

10

11

12a

12b

12c

13

Now for the leaves. As you might expect, thistle leaves are prickly, too. But first, let's make the leaf color and shape before we have to worry about those pokey edges.

8 Time to make the background. Wipe your hands first to get rid of any green residue, then take the pinkish clay blend and run it through the pasta machine at the widest setting. Use a cutting blade to slice it into a cool pin shape—how about a parallelogram? They're awesome! Ok, maybe they're not that awesome, but a long, tall, irregular rectangle will be a nice contrast to the organic lines of the thistle.

9 Smooth the cut edges gently.

10 Lay the thistle on the background however you think it looks good—remember that leaves will be added to the bottom, so don't worry if it looks a bit top-heavy (thistles often do). Once you have it in position, press firmly but gently to attach, and trim off any excess stem.

11 Ooh, the next part is the most fun! Prickles! These are easy. Use the medium-color green clay mix and roll a small lump of it into a teardrop shape with a very thin, sharp point—you'll only need the point, so don't worry about how big the lump is. With a cutting blade, slice off the tip at an angle—about 45°, if you remember your math (wasn't it geometry where we learned about angles? I was busy doodling on my homework paper, so I may have forgotten).

12 To attach the prickle, just put a dot of liquid clay on the roundy part of the thistle (start right below the bristles) and press the prickle onto the liquid clay. See, the angle cut makes the prickle lay right on and point up, just like it should. Wasn't that clever? Keep rolling out points, slice 'em, put on a dot of liquid clay, and press on. See, like that! Make a row along the top. Now do the next row, and keep on, down the roundy part of the flower head and onto the stem a bit as well. Perfect.

13 The basic leaf coloring and shape is simple. Many thistles have a lighter-colored vein running down the middle, and since that will look fun, let's make our leaves like that. Take the lightest-color green and run it through the pasta machine at the widest setting. Set that aside. Now take the darker green and roll it into an oval-shaped cylinder. Slice that cylinder straight through the middle, dividing it into two halves.

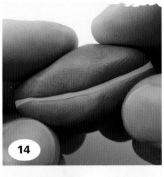

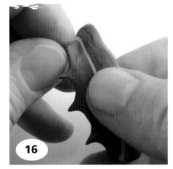

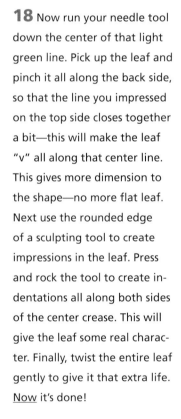

14 Now make a leaf sandwich. Cut the light green clay into a rectangle that is about as long and wide as the inside of that cut-cylinder clay. Slap that slice of clay in between the two halves of cylinder and press them together—see, sandwich. Don't eat it (duh). Trim away any of the light colored "filling" that is peeking out. Press it all together to eliminate any gaps (remember that from the section on making canes—same thing!). You'll be slicing the leaves from this, so now is the time to reduce this simple cane if it seems too large for your thistle.

15 OK, slice! Not too thin, or you'll have droopy leaves. Not too thick, because who wants thick leaves?

16 Now pinch gently all around the outside of the shape just to soften the cut edge and to thin the edge a bit to make the next step easier. Pinch and gently pull the edges to create points. (Remember I told you that even the leaves have prickles? Well, these are them.) Let them be irregular—thick and thin, some a little longer—it's all good. Do this all the way around the shape.

17 OK, that looks kinda boring, huh? But wait, there's more! Now use the edge of a tool and press in notches all around the leaf edge, in between the prickles. Don't make notches on the prickles, just everywhere else.

18 Now run your needle tool down the center of that light green line. Pick up the leaf and pinch it all along the back side, so that the line you impressed on the top side closes together a bit—this will make the leaf "v" all along that center line. This gives more dimension to the shape—no more flat leaf. Next use the rounded edge of a sculpting tool to create impressions in the leaf. Press and rock the tool to create indentations all along both sides of the center crease. This will give the leaf some real character. Finally, twist the entire leaf gently to give it that extra life. <u>Now</u> it's done!

19 Make as many leaves as you need—usually two or three will do the trick—and place them at the bottom of the thistle. Once you like the arrangement, press gently in place.

20 Add some mica powder if you like—pearl color in the center of the flower ball and stem looks nice. Ah, why not a little on the tips of the leaves, too, while you're at it.

The composition is done. Well, OK, there is one more thing that might look nice, if you want to—there's that little bit of background showing that's just kind of bland. Adding a bit of mosaic-like clay would be an interesting contrast, don't you think? Me, too.

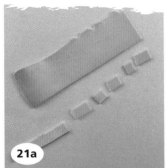

21a

21b

21 Run the background color clay through the pasta machine at a thin setting. Now slice a strip and cut it into little squares. Pick up a square with the tip of a flat tool (wooden ones work best) and place the square on the background clay—it should grab right on. Place on as many as you like to create a nice pattern. There, all done.

Now since this is a going to be a pin, bake it for 15 minutes at 275°F (130°C) just to set it. Let it cool completely, then add the pin back, with liquid clay and new fresh clay. (Need more info? Flip to page 148.)

22 Once the pin back is on, bake for the full time, as usual. Cool completely before adding any finishing touches. Now wear it with pride (but be careful if you hug someone—ouch!).

You can make it smaller, too! Just make everything half-size. Oh, and the stem can just curve if you want, it doesn't have to loop-de-loop.

Finishing Touches

- Patina on the leaves, flower, and stem: use raw sienna and burnt sienna acrylic paints.
- Surface treatment for the background: patina wash, use a lighter blue acrylic paint, such as cerulean blue.
- Clear coating on background is recommended (on flower portion is optional, don't coat the bristles): satin or matte finish.

Grape Expectations
Grapevine Mirror

Size: 4" (10.2 cm)

For this project you will need:

- all the usual sculpting tools
- craft knife or cutting blade
- liquid clay
- 28-gauge craft wire for adding bead embellishments
- raffia: natural color, or assorted brown colors (paper raffia may be used instead)
- embellishment beads: round or drop-shaped stone or glass in grape colors. (These are fluorite.) Size depends on how big you choose to make your mirror. (These are 10mm.)
- mirror: round or oval shape works best. (This one is about 3" [7.6 cm].)
- mica powder (optional): PearlEx 688 Misty Lavender, and paintbrush to apply

Using a mirror in this polymer clay project is easy and a lot of fun. The mirror bakes beautifully, and it gives your art a practical purpose, which is sometimes helpful. When you show this little grapevine mirror to your spouse or friends, you won't have to answer the questions of "What is it?" or "What's it good for?" Obviously, it's a mirror! (Duh!)

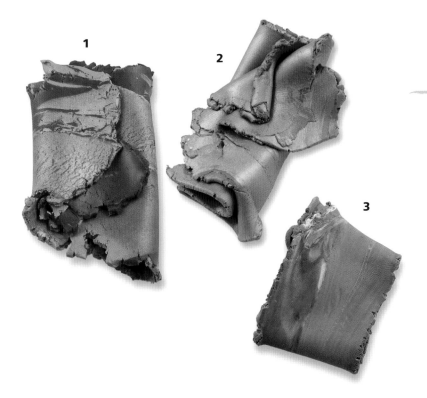

1

2

3

Clay Recipe

1. Vine and mirror covering color:
mix of copper, gold, and burnt umber
(amount: 1 to 2 oz.)

2. Grape color: mix of fuchsia, blue pearl,
white, ecru (amount: 1 oz.)

3. Leaf and tendril color: mix of green
pearl and gold (amount: 0.5 oz.)

Start by mixing clays to create the grapevine color. As you blend, don't over-mix the colors—streaks and clumps will look nicer than one solid brown color. You'll want to make enough of this color to make a nice thick vine, as well as cover the back of the mirror. How much that is depends on the size of the mirror you're using. This mirror is about 3" (7.6 cm) wide, so I mixed up a wad of color about the size of an egg.

1 Set your pasta machine to the middle setting, and roll out the clay mix to form a sheet. Lay your mirror on top and trim the clay all around the mirror about ½" (1.3 cm) or more from the edge of the glass. A cutting blade or craft knife will do the trick.

2 Pick up the mirror and wrap the clay over the edge of the mirror; crimp and press the clay as you go. This will make a clay "frame" all around the mirror, securing the glass, and providing a base for the vines to attach to.

You should have plenty of clay left after cutting off the excess. Take that and wad it up again into a ball. Roll out a nice thick snake from some of that clay wad. Let's figure out how long the snake will need to be: Curl that snake around the outside of the mirror— don't have the clay touch the mirror, just curl around the outside. Rip off the excess— this will give you enough extra clay to accommodate the twists.

3 Now take some raffia—at least three or more strands, and if you have multicolored raffia, use several "viney" colors. (These are natural, brown, and rust-colored strands, in case you were wondering. They just came in these colors in a nice little package.) To hold the clay and raffia together, it's helpful to wrap the end with wire—not too tightly, of course, or it will just slice through the clay, but firmly enough to hold the two materials together.

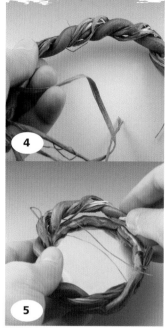

4 OK, twist! Just hold the wired end and twirl the clay and raffia around each other loosely. You want to keep the raffia visible, so don't twist too tightly. With scissors, trim away the excess raffia. Now wrap this end with the wire, too.

5 Next we'll add this clay and raffia vine to the mirror. Since we have raffia as well as clay to connect, it will help to add a little line of liquid clay all around the clay frame of the mirror first. Now place the raffia/clay vine onto the mirror clay and press firmly.

6 Hide one end of the vine by overlapping the other end on top of it. Of course there will be some wires still showing, so use little bits of clay to cover the flaws as well as add to the composition. If they look like small branches or tendrily bits of the vine, it will be more believable. To make those, take a small bit of vine-color clay, shape it into a rice-shaped bit, and twist it. Remember, irregular shapes with lumps and bumps will look more convincing as vines than smooth, perfect shapes. Squeeze and smoosh a little! (It's kinda fun that way, anyway, smoosh, smoosh, smoosh, squish, squish!)

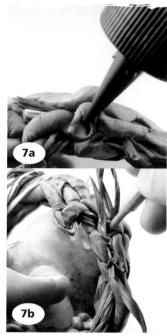

7 Now continue to add little extra vines out of both clay and raffia. The clay is easy, just roll out another snake or rice-shaped bit, twist, and press in place. For the raffia, decide where it's going to go, then poke a hole with a dowel tool in the starting point. Squirt in a bit of liquid clay (this will help grab the raffia when the clay is baked), and use the dowel tool again to press the end of the raffia into the clay/liquid clay as deeply as you can. Once it's in, squeeze the clay to close the hole around the raffia. Now position the raffia as you like over the vine circle, and secure the other end into the clay in the same way. There's no right and wrong here. The idea is just to make this vine look viney, and the raffia will really add that natural feeling.

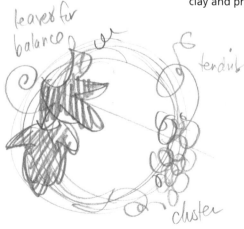

8

10

11

12

It's time to add the grape cluster. First, mix up some grape-colored clay. As you know, grapes come in lots of colors. This grape cluster is bluish-purple because I had some nice, round purple-blue fluorite beads that I wanted to use. You mix your grape-colored clay to match whatever beads you want to use.

8 Pinch off little bits of your grape clay and roll them into little round balls about the same size as your beads. Oh, and while you're at it, roll out some of the grape-colored clay into a thin sheet—more than halfway on the pasta machine dial, roughly ¹⁄₁₆" (1.6 mm) or so. Cut out a "grape cluster" shape. You can shape it with your fingers or cut it out with a blade. This will give the clay balls some support as you stack 'em together.

9 Wire each of your beads, following the directions for wiring single beads on page 146.

10 Gently press those clay balls into a cluster on top of the flat shape you made. Make some of the balls overlap one another. Yup, just like that. Make more balls if you need to, and stack until it looks like a decent cluster. Add the beads here and there, pushing the wire into the clay.

11 Adding a mica powder at this stage is a good idea. It will give the grapes that cool sheen that real grapes have, and dusting the powder on now will keep it from accidentally getting on the clay vine. Use pearl or pearly lavender for the best results (this is PearlEx's Misty Lavender).

12 Add the finished cluster to your vine circle by pressing the cluster on firmly but gently. A bit of liquid clay on the vine underneath the cluster helps to get the grip without having to smush the grapes. They hate that, it makes them wine.

Leaf time! Grape leaves are very distinctive. They have multiple lobes and serrated edges. You do have to incorporate those elements in order to make the grape vine believable. It's a stylized leaf, of course, so it's not necessary to get it perfect, but it should have the look of a grape leaf. If you just stick any ol' leaf shape on there, it will indeed still look like a nice vine, just not really like a grapevine.

▲ Use me as a guide, or trace me and cut me out to use me as a pattern.

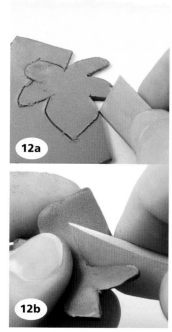

12a

13

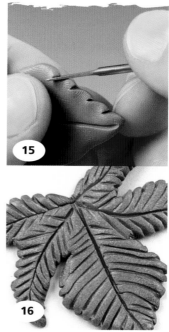

15

17

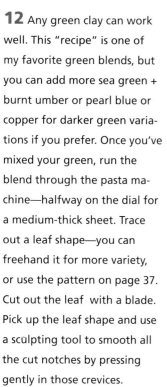

12b

14

16

18

12 Any green clay can work well. This "recipe" is one of my favorite green blends, but you can add more sea green + burnt umber or pearl blue or copper for darker green variations if you prefer. Once you've mixed your green, run the blend through the pasta machine—halfway on the dial for a medium-thick sheet. Trace out a leaf shape—you can freehand it for more variety, or use the pattern on page 37. Cut out the leaf with a blade. Pick up the leaf shape and use a sculpting tool to smooth all the cut notches by pressing gently in those crevices.

13 Continue creating the leaf by using your fingers to pinch all around the edges to eliminate that boring "cookie cutter" look. The pinches add some "realistic" irregularity to the edges.

14 Lay the leaf back down and now add the veins by impressing the lines with a needle tool—hold the needle almost parallel to the clay, for a clean, line. Start with the center line straight down through the middle of the leaf. Now make a line from the top through the center of each lobe. They won't be straight lines, since the leaf lobes curve, so don't stress! All the lines start at the top, like umbrella spokes.

15 OK, now for those serrated edges that grape leaves have (look it up, you'll see!). Use any tool with a flat edge. Press the tool into the edge of the leaf, creating a notch. Do this all the way around. Press upward so the little points face downward.

16 All that's left is to impress the little veins into the leaf from the center veins to the other edges. (Take a look at that pattern leaf on the previous page again if it gets confusing!)

17 As a final touch to add some fun liveliness to the leaf, pick it up and pinch the back along the middle line—cool, huh? Makes it look almost real, doesn't it?

18 Attach the leaf onto the vine by pressing the leaf with the edge of a tool—use a tool that's doesn't have too sharp of an edge, and rock back and forth just a little while you press. This way is better than using your finger, since it will help to keep from smooshing any of those little veins that took so long to create. Curl the leaf edges for maximum fabulousness.

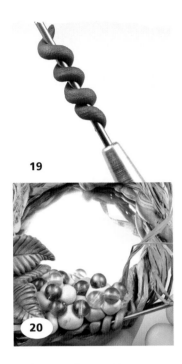

19

20

Make more leaves. You can use the same pattern, just cut a little more off here, stretch slightly there, and each leaf will look different enough. Press them on, too. It always looks better to press a few closer together in balanced clumps, rather than space the leaves out equally along the vine.

19 Once you've made enough leaves, here's one last grapevine touch—little green tendrils. They're easy. Just take a little of your green leaf clay, roll out a thin snake, and wrap it around a needle tool.

20 Press the snake, still on the tool, into the clay of the vine. Give the tool a little twist to break the "grip" of the clay, and slowly slide the tool out of the coil. Tah-dah!

And you're done!
Bake as usual.

TIP: If you worry about the raffia cracking during baking and becoming too brittle, you can brush it with a very light coating of liquid clay, especially on the cut edges. (Remove any excess with a cotton swab or tissue.) A bit of vegetable oil brushed on after baking instead will accomplish the same thing.

Finishing Touches

- Patina only the leaves: use burnt sienna.
- Don't add a clear coating—keep it natural, with the exception of the clay part of the grapes. They can get a clear coating of satin or matte finish.

Let It Snow!
Holly Berry Cluster Gift Tag

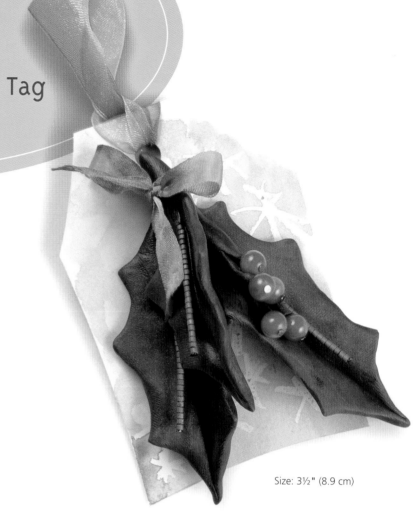

Size: 3½" (8.9 cm)

For this project you will need:

- all the usual sculpting tools
- craft knife
- needle tool
- headpins: 2" (5.1 cm) long are best, and in a darker color, such as antique brass
- wire for the stringing channel: 16-gauge or thicker
- paper tag (or Bristol board/card stock to create tag; hole punch for the hole)
- white china pencil
- ribbon (this is hand-dyed silk)
- blue watercolor (with large, soft brush to apply)
- coral beads (or glass in similar orange-red color): 6–8 mm
- green seed beads

When that holiday gift-giving season comes around each year, it's always nice to have a way to make those special gifts really look festive. Here's a cheery winter holly cluster gift tag that's sure to get noticed!

1

Clay Recipe

1. Holly leaf clay = sea green + burnt umber + green pearl (about three parts sea green + burnt umber to one part pearl green) (amount: 1 to 1.5 oz.)

2

3

4

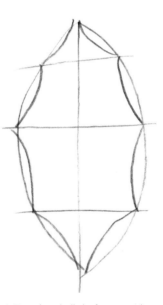

1 Start with a paper tag, of course. You can find one premade anywhere that papers and scrapbooking supplies are sold. If you'd like to make your own, I suggest a slightly irregular shape to add some personality. Use stiff paper—Bristol board is ideal, but card stock will work fine, too. A classic tag shape is just a rectangle with shoulders—cut out the rectangle, then snip off the top corners. Use a hole punch in the center of the top.

2 To create an icy-licious snowflake pattern, use a china pencil and draw quick, free-form asterisks (these things: *), they work great!

3 You may have noticed that you just used a white pencil to draw on white paper. So now we need to add a water-color wash to reveal the white snowflakes. (This is why you use a china pencil—it's water-resistant. You can use a white crayon too, with the same result). Watercolors work best—mix up a blue with enough water for the paint to be nice and sloppy, but still intense. Use a big, soft brush and swipe the color right over the tag in one go. The snowflakes will pop right out—nifty, huh? Let the tag dry.

4 Cut out the holly leaf pattern. Roll out the green clay at the widest setting on the pasta machine and lay the pattern on top. Use a craft blade to cut out the clay around the pattern.

▲ To make a holly leaf pattern, draw a classic leaf (the almond shape) and run a line straight down the middle. Now draw three horizontal lines across the leaf. Draw scallop swoops from line to line—tah-dah! A holly leaf! Or just trace out this one and use it!

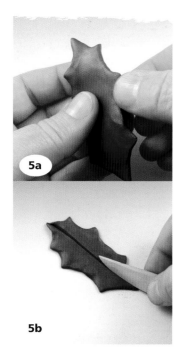

5a

5b

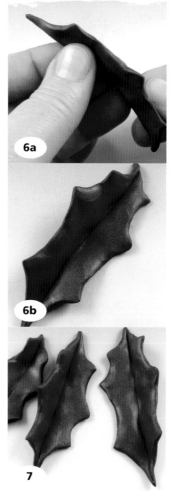

6a

6b

7

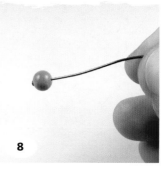

8

9

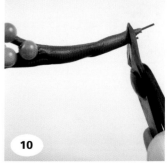

10

5 Peel off the pattern, pick up the clay, and pinch all along the edges. This will eliminate the "cookie cutter" look (icky—cookie cutter look bad!). Now set it down, and use the edge of a tool to embed a line down the middle— this line should go at least halfway through the clay (we'll use it as a fold line soon).

6 OK, it's soon … now. Pick up the leaf and pinch it on the backside, all along the line you just made. That's it. Holly leaf!

7 This project will look best with a cluster of three leaves. It's also nice to make them different sizes. Just trim the pattern down first, then repeat steps 4 to 6.

8 If you've ever looked at a holly plant to examine the berries (well, I don't know, you might have!), you may have noticed that each orange-red berry has a dark brown dot (left over from the blossom, no doubt). It's a rather distinctive aspect to the holly berry, and if we duplicate it in this project, it will really add to the believability of the look. Luckily, there's a really easy way to do this—it's almost like cheating! (Which of course is absolutely acceptable in the world of creating—anything that makes it easier to get the look you want is groovy!) Use a dark headpin (an antique brass or antique copper works fabulously) and slip on the bead—instant berry!

9 Wrap the wire of the holly berry with some of the green clay. You can roll out a log, run it through the pasta machine at a thin setting, then wrap it around the wire. Press, twist, and pinch away any excess until you have a nice clay casing around the wire. This will hold the bead berry in place and make the wire look properly like a stem.

10 Now make more berries— a berry cluster—and press all the clay-wrapped stems together, they'll clump in a nice little bunch. Use wire cutters to snip off the ends, and make them flush. Pull the clay over the wire ends. Now set that aside for a bit.

11a

11b

12a

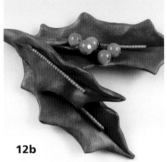

12b

13a

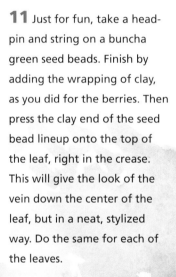

13b

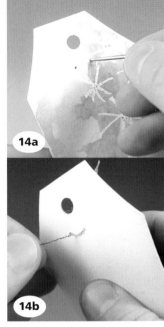

14a

14b

11 Just for fun, take a head-pin and string on a buncha green seed beads. Finish by adding the wrapping of clay, as you did for the berries. Then press the clay end of the seed bead lineup onto the top of the leaf, right in the crease. This will give the look of the vein down the center of the leaf, but in a neat, stylized way. Do the same for each of the leaves.

12 Now press two of the leaves together to join. Add the other leaf, and the berry cluster on top of that. How jolly! A holly cluster!

Before you bake it, pierce a hole in the stem, and slip in a thicker piece of wire to hold open a channel for the ribbon that will be added later. Now bake in the usual way.

13 The holly cluster will look just right with a nice bow. First pull a ribbon through the stringing hole (you remembered to pull out the wire first, right? Hee hee). Now tie a lovely little bow! Next, slip a piece of 28-gauge wire through the hole, under the ribbon.

14 To add the cluster to the tag, first poke two holes side by side, near the top. Insert the wires from the holly stem through the holes and twist the ends together, tightly against the paper. Snip off the excess ends of the wire. Tape down the ends against the paper.

And that's that! Of course, since it's such an awesome gift tag, make sure the person whose gift it will adorn knows you made it special!

Finishing Touches

- Patina of darker browns: burnt sienna and/or burnt umber acrylic paints.

Funky Flowers
Glass-Centered Flower Beads

Size: ¾" to 2" (1.9 to 5 cm)

For this project you will need:

- all the usual scultpting tools
- dowel tools
- round-nose pliers
- headpins: any color, 2" (5 cm), preferably
- lampwork glass beads: (flattish ones recommended) assorted sizes and colors
- additional accent beads: bicone crystal, dagger beads, etc.
- mica powders, to match (optional)
- ribbons in assorted greens
- 28-gauge wire
- wire for the stringing channel: 16-gauge or thicker
- assorted ribbons and braids

Are ya feelin' a little funky? (Don't worry, that's a good thing). Here are some very easy, very funky flowers to go with that attitude.

The centers of these flowers are lampwork glass beads. I chose ones that were flat—like buttons. (Hey, that's an idea—you could use metal or shell or glass buttons for the centers on the next batch!)

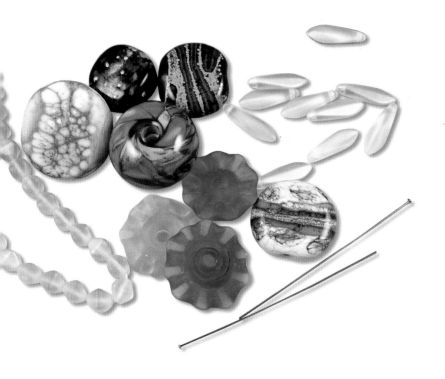

Clay Recipe

No clay recipes for this project! Let the lampwork glass beads you use determine the color of the flowers. Use lots of ecru or white to keep the colors in the pastel range (use ecru for earthy pastels, white for brighter pastels). It'll be fun—experiment!

Begin by mixing up clays to go with the beads you chose. Get funky with the color mixing, too—let the bead inspire the color. I mixed the clays to create pastel colors in brighter, happy tones. (amount: 0.5 oz. per flower)

1

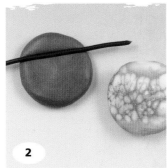

2

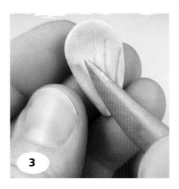

3

4

1 From your color mixes, roll out little balls of clay to become the petals—how many will be determined by how wide you like your petals, but about the size of an almond is a good start. Roll each ball into a teardrop shape, then flatten the teardrops with your fingers. Curve the fat end of the teardrop over a fingertip to make it cup. That's nicer-looking than a flat petal, don't you think?

2 Pick a green, any green—clay, that is—and roll it into a ball and smoosh it flat. That's the base for your petals. It should be about the same size as the bead that you chose for the center. Now lay a piece of thick wire down on top of the clay toward the top, not in the middle, so the finished bead will hang properly. Otherwise gravity will have its way and the bead will tip forward and hang all floppy). Roll out a small snake of the same green clay and press it on top of the wire, sandwiching the wire inside.

3 Back to the petals—for interest, press some lines into the petals with the edge of a tool.

4 Lay the petals onto the green clay pad—pointy ends in, round ends out, duh! Press them down firmly to attach them to the middle of the green clay pad.

5

7

8

6

7 For a last bit of fun, dust the center of the flower with mica powders, something that will go good with the colors of the clay and the bead. You can dust the center of the flower, or the tips of the petals. Or both, with different colors of powder!

5 Now this next step is optional (but it looks good, so do it!). Roll out some little snakes of clay in a contrasting color and position them in the center of each petal. Press the ends in the center to attach. Doesn't that look fun?

6 Wire up the lampwork glass bead in the usual way, but since it's bigger, make sure to bend in a little hooky-thing at the end for extra grab. Press the bead, wire side first, into the center of the clay. Press down firmly to make sure it embeds into the clay.

8 To hold the "bowl" shape of the flower while it waits for its companions to be made, make a little doughnut of tissue or toilet paper, set the flower in the middle, and see—doesn't that prop up the petals nicely! (And it's okay to bake it with the paper.)

Floral Inspiration

These flower beads weren't the result of an interesting doodle, but were inspired by the glass flowers of Nanette Young-Greiner (her website info is in the Reference section at the back of the book). The classy simplicity and happy colors just begged to be translated into polymer clay!

1

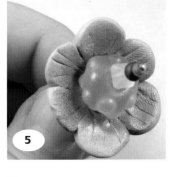

5

Are you ready for funky bead number two? Of course you are!

1 Begin by slipping several beads onto a long headpin—I suggest a seed bead first, then a slightly larger bead or two, then a lampworked one. Hold the end of the headpin close to the last bead with a pair of round-nose pliers and wrap the wire around the pliers to make a loop.

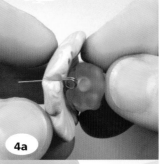

2a

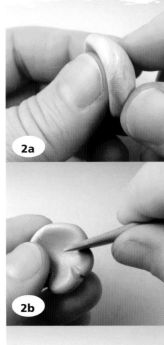

2b

3

2 Next let's make the petal cup for the beads to sit in. Roll clay into a ball, then form it around your finger into a cup shape (if you have long nails, go find someone else's fingers to use). With the edge of a tool, impress notches along the rim of the cup to create the petals. Press in deep and smooth—yup, just like that.

3 A few more of those lines in the center of the petals would be ever so funky.

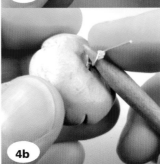

4a

4b

4 Add the beaded headpin by just pressing the wire into the center of the cup. Pull it all the way through, loop part and all, until the bead rests firmly against the clay, and all the wire bits are sticking out the back. Now insert the tip of a dowel tool into the wire loop out the back, so you can hold the beaded headpin tight and steady while you firm up all the clay on the backside of the flower (the hole gets a little sloppy when you put the wire in, and needs to be patched up, so just smooth it with fingers or tool).

5 Finesse the petals—press and shape them, now that all the construction is over with. Add mica powders to the center, and voila! All done!

Three's the charm, right? So one more flower design to make three!

1 The petals for this one aren't clay, but dagger beads—gotta shake things up a little, ya know. Slip enough dagger beads onto a piece of the 28-gauge wire for them to form a nice circle. Pull the wire ends together and twist them with the pliers. Snip off the excess wire to leave the twisted tail about ¼" (6 mm) long. Bend a hook in the end of the wire. Now bend that wire with the hook at a 90 degree angle, so that it will stick straight into the clay when the ring of beads is pressed on.

2 For the petal ring to have something to hold on to, make a pad of clay. Secure a thicker wire to the clay pad as in step 2 on page 45. Now firmly press the ring of beads into the center of this clay pad, embedding the twisted wire tail.

3 Cover the center opening of the ring of beads with a small, flattened circle of clay pressed firmly into place. Use an interesting contrasting color of clay.

4 Wire up and press in a bead center in the same way as you did for funky bead number two. (For this I used a funky glass bead, since it's a funky bead day!)

Make more flowers until you get bored of them! Experiment a little—what if the clay petals were pointier? How would a layer of clay petals underneath the layer of dagger bead petals look? (Do the clay ones first and press the dagger bead circle on top.) Maybe a double-cup flower. You know, get funky with it!

Once they're done, bake them all in the usual way. (Don't forget to cushion the beads with tissue paper if you need to prop up petals or support shapes.)

Finishing Touches

- Patina carefully; don't let the paint clump up and darken the flowers too much. Use lighter browns for earthy tones, or patina with other colors—perhaps an orange patina on the yellow flower, or a purple patina on the sky blue one.
- Clear coat on the clay (don't coat the beads, of course). For earthy-toned flowers, use a satin or matte finish; for brighter colors, use a higher-gloss finish if you prefer.

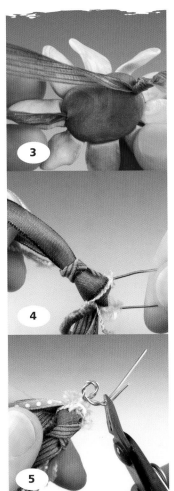

What to do with funky flower beads? Hmmm, well, obviously, you can string one of them up as the focal bead of a necklace. Or you can string a bunch of them up as a necklace bouquet! Or how about this—give several of the flowers a hanging ribbon and festoon a glass vase with them! Here's how:

1 Remove the heavy wire and string the ribbon through the funky flower bead.

2 You can measure approximately how much you'll need by draping the ribboned bead loosely around the neck of the vase and grabbing the ribbon there to hold the spot. Now knot the tails together.

3 Slide the ribbon through the hole until the knot stops at the edge of the flower. Next, snip off the dangling ribbons to a nice length.

Pull through and knot the ribbon hangers onto several flower beads in the same way. Set them aside for now.

4 Take a cluster of ribbons, tie a knot in the middle and slip a wire through the center of the knot (at least a 22-gauge or thicker works best).

5 With pliers, twist a loop close to the knot. Snip off any excess wire.

6 Now slip another ribbon through the loop, tie that ribbon around the neck of the vase, and slide the knot to the front to dangle with its fellow ribbons. Drape the funky flowers over the lip of the vase, on top of the ribbon cluster, and arrange 'em!

Stand this vase alone as a little art piece or pour some water in the vase, arrange in a little greenery—leaves and twigs and ferns and whatnot—and you'll be quite the artsy-fartsy with the flowers on the outside of the vase and the greens on the inside! (And you know you always wanted to be artsy. I'm not so sure about the fartsy, though.)

Love 'Em and Leaf 'Em
Leaf and Flower Designs

Size: 2" (5.1 cm)

Size: 4½" (11.4 cm)

For this project you will need:

- all the usual sculpting tools
- cutting blade
- accents: these are pearls, carnelian beads, fossilized coral cabochon, enameled beads, disks, and rings
- beading cable in a thin size: this is Beadalon 49 strand size 0.013"; you can also use size 0.015"
- crimp beads and crimp covers
- crimping pliers
- liquid clay
- 28-gauge craft wire
- headpins: any color or size (I used antique copper)
- wire for the stringing channel: 16-gauge or thicker
- mica powder (I used PearlEx 689 Blue Russet)

If you want to spend a fun afternoon creating, all you need to do is make these clay leaves and then arrange them into clusters. You'll be amazed how much variety you can achieve with a minimal amount of tricks (and how delightfully fun it is!). OK, I'll prove it—let's make completely different-looking leafy pendant pieces using the same clay colors and the same choices of accent beads. The first one will be an "urban jungle" pendant— tropical but contemporary. The other will be a simple and sweet posy.

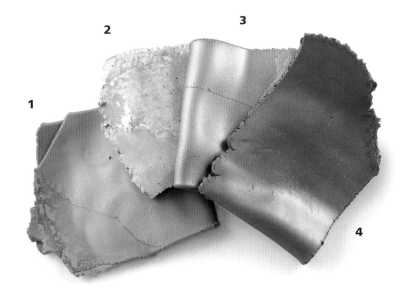

Clay Recipe

Several shades of green—any three or four that look good together will work. These are:

1. Green pearl + ultramarine blue + ecru (just a bit more green than blue and only a smidgen of ecru) (amount: 0.5 to 1 oz.)

2. Green pearl + ecru + Cernit Nature Color agate (equal parts green pearl and agate with just a little ecru) (amount: 0.5 to 1 oz.)

3. Green pearl + gold (equal parts of each) (amount: 0.5 to 1 oz.)

4. Green pearl + copper (two parts green to one part copper) (amount: 0.5 to 1 oz.)

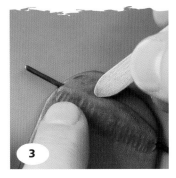

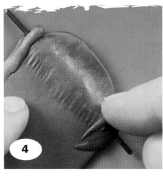

1 Start with the darkest of your green and run it through the pasta machine. Cut out a nice pendant shape, like an oval.

2 Now use your fingers to smooth the cut edge all around—we don't want a "cookie cutter" look, that's tacky!

3 Lay a 2" to 3" (5 to 7.6 cm) piece of the thicker wire on the clay, at the top of the pendant shape. Roll out a little snake of clay from the same color, flatten it a bit in your fingers and lay it on top of the wire, from edge to edge, completely covering it. Now smooth that snake into the pendant clay. The wire will hold open a stringing channel while you sculpt so you don't have to think about it. Isn't that nice?

4 Of course, that edge where the wire comes out looks a little unfinished. We can't have that. Roll out two little snakes of clay and drape them over the wires and press them firmly into the sides and/or top of the pendant base. Smooth the ends onto the pendant. You can leave the tops of the snake loop unblended if you want to—they'll look like vines anyway, if they aren't covered up by leaves later.

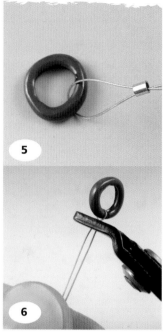

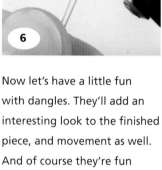

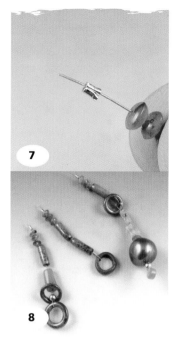

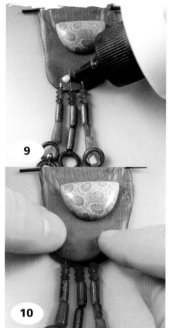

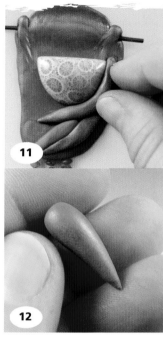

Now let's have a little fun with dangles. They'll add an interesting look to the finished piece, and movement as well. And of course they're fun to make.

5 Start by snipping off a bit of the flexible beading wire. There are several brands out there—this is Beadalon 49-strand 24-karat gold-covered wire. I love this stuff! It's very flexible, and of course, it's gold—can't go wrong there.

Loop the cable around one of the rings and slide on the crimp bead. (Don't forget there's more info on crimping on page 149 in case this is an unfamiliar process to you.)

6 Squeeze the crimp with your crimping pliers and complete the crimp.

7 The completed crimp is usually less than lovely and should be covered up with something nicer—like a crimp cover, or a bead that has a large hole so it can slip over the crimp. Once you've prettied the crimp, add some additional beads—about 1" (2.5 cm) or so will do it. Now add a final crimping bead and crimp it into place so that it doesn't slip. Leave about ¼" (6 mm) or more of beading wire showing above the beads, before the crimp. No need to cover this crimp—it'll get covered by clay, so we won't have to look at it.

8 Make at least three dangles. Vary their lengths a bit, too.

9 We're going to add the dangles directly to the clay and bake them in place—that way, they will be very secure. Lay the uncovered crimp directly onto the clay at the bottom of the pendant. Now add a thin line of liquid clay on top (the liquid clay will bake all around the crimp, ensuring that it will be firmly attached).

10 Now cover up the ends with a flattened snake of clay (use the same color as the pendant). Press it into place and smooth that clay into the pendant the same way as you did for the stinging-channel-wire clay.

Did you notice I snuck a cabochon onto the piece when you weren't looking? Sneaky, huh? Typically, a cabochon is a flat based piece of glass, stone, or ceramic without a hole drilled into it. You can add it to clay

by using the clay to hold it in place. It's better if you can add the clay in such a way that it's not readily noticeable that the clay is being functional. It should just flow with the design. The best way to do this is to start adding the clay at the bottom of the pendant and make it flow up and around the edge of the cabochon. It will look good and hold the piece in place.

11 Just use simple snakes of clay, flattened slightly, and overlapping each other. Use more than one of the green colors, too, just for fun.

I promised you leaves, so let's make some of those now, to go with the snakes in wrapping around the cabochon.

12 Roll out a teardrop shape.

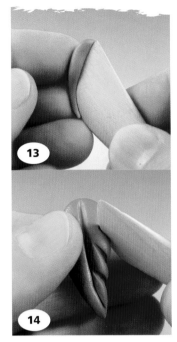

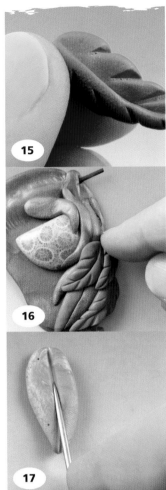

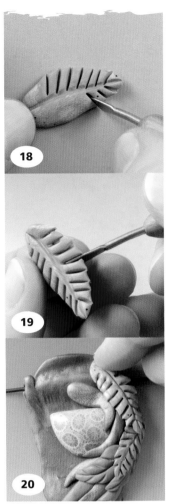

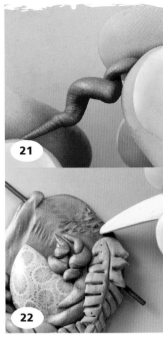

13 Use a tool with a gently curved edge and press it down into the middle of the teardrop. This will flatten one side and create a centerline as well. Pinch the edges of the leaf a bit, too, so it won't be too fat and blobby. No one wants that.

14 Remember that whole ramble at the beginning of the chapter about "stylizing"? Well, this is definitely going to be a stylized leaf—the form and feel of a leaf, simplified instead of ultra-realistic. To stylize the veins of a leaf, simply press the sharp edge of your tool into the edge of the leaf shape. I find it helpful to press the tool into the edge and then continue to roll the blade toward that center line. Make the lines angling up, too.

15 Do the same to the other side, also angling up. There you go—one artsy, stylized leaf.

16 Make some more. See, didn't I tell you making leaves was a fun way to spend some time? Add them to the pendant, following the flow around the cabochon. Add more snakes, too, for contrast if you want.

17 OK, how about one more leaf for contrast (and because I did promise "leaves," not "leaf")? Roll out another teardrop (use a different green color) and flatten it a bit with your fingers. Impress a line down the center with any pointy tool.

18 Slice notches into both sides of the leaf shape—angle each upward again.

19 Now smooth those cuts with the blade of a tool. There will probably be jaggedy bits that look very un-leaflike, so clean 'em up!

20 Add those leaves, too, wherever you want.

21 Hey, how about some tendrils? Those always look good, and they'll be a good contrast to the leaves in color and shape. Plus, they can help hold in the cabochon on the other side (we can't leave that open or the cab will slip out). Roll out a little snake of clay and twist. (We did these for the grapevine mirror on page 36, remember?)

22 Press them in place. I did some in lighter green as well as the browner green. If you allow the tips of the tendrils to stick out past the pendant shape (which does look good), make sure not to let them stick out too far—those little points are more fragile and prone to being snagged or broken off.

Now use a pointy tool to rough up the background clay at the top. This will make it look like bark or moss or something organic.

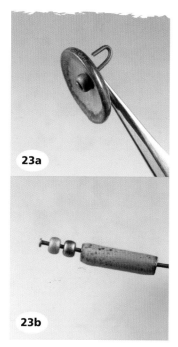

23a

23b

23 Wire up pearls or other accent beads. Put some of the pieces (like this enamel disk and enamel tube bead) on headpins along with seed beads. Trim the headpin and bend over the end.

24

24 Add all the accent beads and any leaves needed to make the design look complete. I clustered the disks and pearl at the top to mimic a floral look. These "flowers" would definitely grow in an urban jungle, don't you think? I added the enamel tube and carnelian drops at the bottom to go with the flow of those bottom leaves.

Make sure everything is pressed in securely. Bake in the usual way

Wanna make another? This one will use the same colors, the same leaf, and the same accents to make a completely different-looking pendant—the posy version.

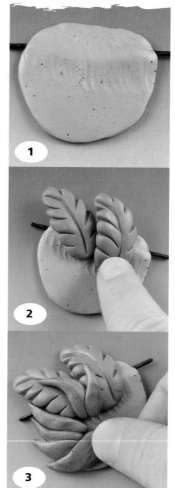

1

2

3

1 Start with a pendant base again—roll out clay, cut out the shape, and smooth it with your fingers. Lay the thicker wire on top, cover it with a flattened snake of clay, and smooth that snake onto the pendant clay.

2 Now make some of those stylized leaves just like we did for the jungle piece. You can make them a little fatter and stouter if you'd like. Press some in place on top of the pendant base.

3 Slam on a few flattened snakes of clay for contrast.

4

5a

5b

4 Use the tool to rough up the visible base clay to mimic moss again—see, same tricks so far!

5 Add some accents—I used the same enameled rings—but instead of making a dangle, how about just wrapping the wire around so the ring can just press into place among the leaves? Hey, how about another ring accent? Wire it up and press it in, too. Swell!

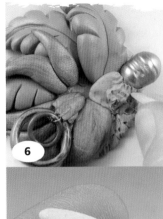

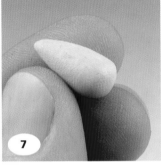

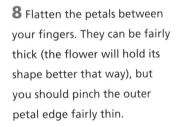

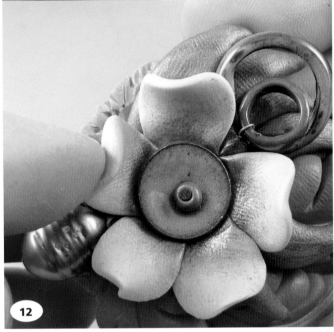

6 One of those pearls would work next. Wire it up, press it in. Because some of its wire was showing, I added a bit more clay to cover it and roughed that up, too—the moss is growing on the pearl.

7 I feel the need for a flower, don't you? This can be any color you like. I chose a light blue just because. To make the petals, roll out five small balls of clay and form them into teardrops.

8 Flatten the petals between your fingers. They can be fairly thick (the flower will hold its shape better that way), but you should pinch the outer petal edge fairly thin.

9 Add the petals in a circle in that spot we left open just for them.

10 Remember the disk bead on headpin from the first piece? Do that trick again and press it right into the center of the flower. Doesn't that look interesting?

11 OK, interesting, but it still needs something. When in doubt, add a touch of powder! Gently dust the clay all around the disk. I chose a deep burgundy color because there were hints of that in the enamel disk already. Use a large, soft brush and remember a little goes a long way, so use a light touch!

12 Wanna hear a secret about how to make a nice flower into an awesome flower? Just press a dip into the edge of each petal. Nice and easy. Pretty nifty, huh? Now bake as usual.

So, what do you think? Ready to spend the rest of the day making leaves and flowers and grouping them into fun little clusters? I thought so.

Creature Feature

Animals, Birds, and Other Living Things

Oh, animals are fun to create! Just like creating plant designs, creating animal designs will give you a wonderful variety in texture, color, and shapes.

As we try to capture the personality of each animal in these following projects, we will sometimes be cute, sometimes be sophisticated, and sometimes be quirky. Of course, this is nothing new in the world of art. Animals have been stylized in everything from the ancient paintings of bison on the walls of the caves in Lascaux to the latest manga cartoons fresh from Tokyopop (yeah, I've got a teenager into all that).

So, on to the main feature—creatures!

Porcupine Mini Scuplture, *page 74*

Flying Bird Focal Bead, *page 66*

Gecko Sculpture, *page 80*

Panda in Bamboo Wrist Cuff, *page 58*

Peek-A-Boo!

Panda in Bamboo Wrist Cuff

Size: 2" (5.1 cm) wide

For this project you will need:

- all the usual sculpting tools
- needle tool
- metal cuff
- pearls: flat, "biwa" style, preferably bottom-drilled (you can substitute any flat, narrow bead that would make nice leaves)
- glass micro beads (also called holeless beads): in black and clear
- two 3mm or 4mm round dark beads (garnet works especially nicely for this project)
- liquid clay
- small, soft-bristle paintbrush (a watercolor brush, or similar)
- heat gun (optional, but helpful!)

So far in this book, we've had great fun with plants, haven't we? So now let's ease into this next section on animal projects by making a design that's half plant and half animal. I'm sure you'll probably think of ways to combine the bamboo you'll be making with some of the other jungley things you've already made. And the panda part, well ... you may find yourself making more of them, too!

1 2 3 4

Clay Recipe

1. Panda face white = white + pearl + ecru—equal parts white and pearl, then to that mix, add one part of ecru to four or five part ratio of the white/pearl—this should make a slightly ivory white (amount: 1 oz.)

2. Panda black = black + ultramarine blue—two parts black to one part blue (this is a richer, friendlier color than just plain ol' black) (amount: 1 oz.)

3. Lighter green for the bamboo = green pearl + fluorescent green + ecru + dark ochre—about three-quarters of this should be the greens, with the ecru and ochre making up the other part (and more ecru than ochre). If you don't have ochre use a smidgen of gold instead (amount: 2 oz.)

4. Darker green for the cuff = green pearl + green + burnt umber + smidgen of yellow—mostly green pearl and green, with enough burnt umber to darken it for contrast to the bamboo color mix (amount: 2 oz.)

Mix the clay colors (do the white mix first, then the green, and finally the black, so the black won't muck up the other colors).

Cuff Stuff

You can find metal cuffs at many stores that offer jewelry supplies. Any metal will do, the lighter the weight the better. Squeeze the cuff to bend it to fit your wrist before you start to add the clay—it won't bend to change its size after the clay is baked on.

In order for the cuff to easily slip onto your wrist, the opening has to be large enough. Of course, this sometimes makes it easy for the cuff to fall off as well. To help keep the cuff secure, after step 6 you can add wire loops under the bamboo. Make a loop in the same way as a pendant loop (see page 148), lay the loops—one on each side—on top of the dark green clay of the cuff, and cover them with a little flattened ball of clay. This will make sure they're on securely. Then continue with step 7. Once the cuff is all done, you can add jump rings and clasps.

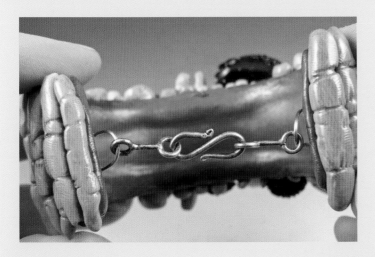

Fun fact: Bamboo makes up 99% of a panda's diet. Pandas can eat up to 40 pounds of it in a day—bamboo juice, bamboo stew, bamboo casserole…

1

1 The bamboo green is a nice medium green, but you'll want to have some variations to give your bamboo lineup some visual depth and variety. I suggest cutting it in half. Set half aside as is, and then add more ecru to the other half, making a lighter version. Now cut that in half and add more ecru to one half, making an even lighter version. This will give you some good bamboo options.

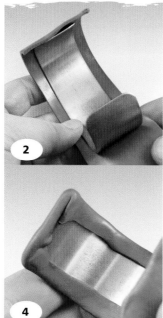

2

4

2 Roll your darker green clay through the pasta machine at a medium-wide setting. Lay it down and cut out a strip a little wider and longer than the cuff (a little less than ½" [1.3 cm] on each side and end should do the trick).

3 Before you add this to the cuff, you'll need another strip—shorter and narrower—to cover the inside of the cuff. I suggest that you lay the first strip on a piece of paper and trace it. Remove the clay, and draw a line about ½" (1.3 cm) inside the traced line. Cut it out on that new line and use to pattern to cut the inside strip. Set that one aside for the moment.

4 Now pick up the wider strip and press it over the metal, folding the sides over as you go. Press the sides firmly all around.

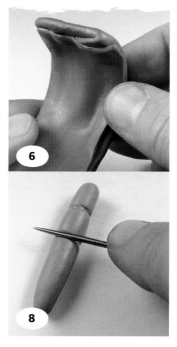

6

8

5 Grab that other strip of clay you made and slap that onto the underside. It should overlap the clay that folded over from the top of the cuff. Groovy.

6 Blend the underneath clay smoothly with fingers or tool, to make it seamless—it should look like a green clay cuff. When you're done, set it aside for now; it's time to make a bunch of bamboo!

7 Grab a bit of one of the light greens—doesn't matter which one—and roll out a little log of clay just a little longer than the cuff is wide.

8 Use a needle tool, and roll the length of it onto the log to create a line going all the way around (like a ring on a finger). Make several of these rings—anywhere from three to five of them will look best.

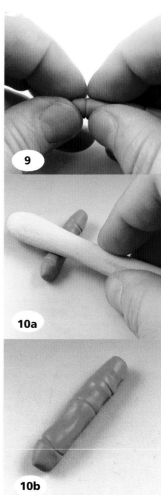

9

10a

10b

9 Now push the clay together from both directions, toward the ring. This will cause the space to close up, and the clay to bunch up a little on either side of the ring line.

10 Now use any tool that has a nice, wide, round handle and push it over the clay in between the lines, rolling the log as if you were rolling clay into a log shape, but with the tool instead of your fingers. This will emphasize the indentations between the lines, making this look like bamboo.

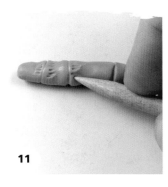

11

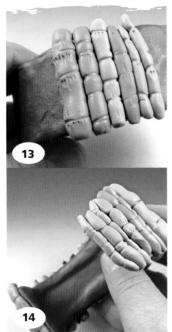

13

14

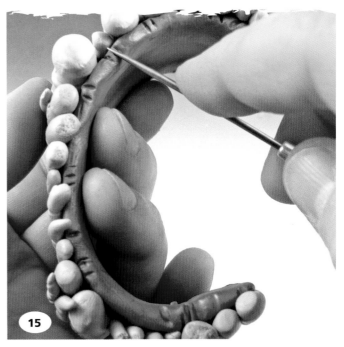

15

11 Well, almost believable. It needs one more thing. Impress little lines on both sides of the lines, mimicking the look of the real thing. Yup, just like that.

12 OK, now make a whole rainforest of little bamboo bits. Use all three of the greens you mixed for this and vary the lengths and thicknesses so your forest will look more natural. Also vary how many lines you impress in each one; some more and some less. (The thicker ones look better with less, and the thin ones look better with more, in case you were wondering.)

13 Now press them onto the cuff. Just lay them in place, and gently but firmly press to attach. Start in the center and work your way around (this way you can set the cuff down on its ends if you need a break, without damaging the tips of the bamboo).

14 When you get to the ends, make sure the bamboo covers the darker green clay. And you're done.

15 OK, you're not done—just kidding! At this point I think it looks nice to use the edge of a tool and impress lines all along the edge of the cuff—that dark green clay on top and bottom—to continue the feel of the ridges. It makes the cuff background feel like a part of the whole, not just a background.

16 Set the cuff down on a little cushioning wad of tissues, to keep everything from getting smooshed.

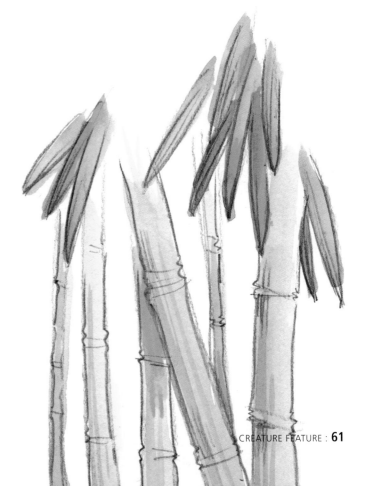

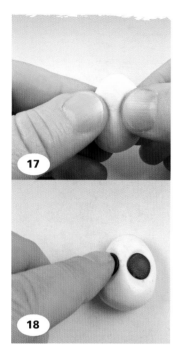

17

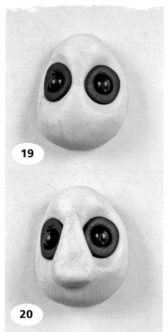

19

20

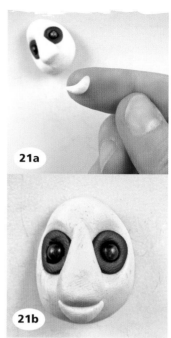

21a

21b

22

23

24

Right about now would be a great time to take a break, stretch, and get a snack so you'll have lots of energy for the next part. (I recommend a bite of chocolate. OK, two bites—just to stimulate creativity, of course.)

17 On to the panda. Start by rolling out a little ball of the white clay mix for the head, about the size of a grape. Use your thumbs to impress two indentations for eye sockets.

18 Now roll out two little balls of the black clay mix—about the size of BBs—and press them into the center of the indentations. Flatten them as you press them in place, so that they look like pancakes.

19 Wire up two beads for eyes (I recommend 4mm round garnets) and smush them into the centers of the black pancakes, embedding them halfway into the clay (no popeyed pandas, please).

20 Make sure you clean your hands each time you go from touching the black clay to touching the white clay, or else your panda will look all bruised from the black clay residue. The bridge of the nose/cheeks is just a simple teardrop shape, pressed on between the eyes.

21 The lips/chin is also a simple shape—a rice-shaped bit, curved like a smile, appropriately enough. Just tuck it into place below the nose/cheek teardrop.

22 Now the nose. You know, the little black part. Obviously use the black clay, roll out a little bit (about the size you did for the eyes), and press it into a flattish triangle shape. Your fingers will easily make the triangle shape, but then press that shape flatter, so his nose won't stick out too far!

23 Press it on!

24 Back to the black clay for the ears. Roll out balls of clay (about a quarter of the size that you rolled out for the head at the beginning). Now make them egg-shaped and flatten them slightly. With your blade, slice off the narrower ends so that they will lay right on the head nicely. I find it easiest to lay them beside the head, in the place they will go, and then cut parallel to the head. That way I don't have to remember which way the cut should go, I can just see it.

25

26

27

28

29

31

32

31 Now press them into place, wire side first. Make sure you really press the pearls in deeply at the wire end, and press them flat against the bamboo—embed them into the bamboo a bit, actually. Pearls are fragile and you don't want any sticking out where they can get accidentally nicked or broken off.

32 Use little bits of the bamboo clay mix to make little snakes of clay as branches to lay on top of the pearls, to create some realism. You want the pearls to look like they grew out of the bamboo, not that they were just pressed on top. As long as the clay branches are connected to the clay of the bamboo, they will stay on top of the pearls just fine.

25 Press the ears on firmly, no need to blend anything.

26 To add the head to the cuff, I suggest adding a drop of liquid clay to the intended spot first. That way, you can place the head on, wiggle it around a little to get the liquid clay to "gum up," and then press gently all around. This will make a firm join, with minimal smooshing!

27 OK, we're on the home stretch! The arm is easy. Roll out a log from the black clay and taper the ends. Now bend it gently like a big parenthesis shape and flatten it slightly.

28 Use the liquid clay trick again, and press the arm into position under the head.

29 Add some claws at the front of the arm. Roll out little black rice-shaped bits, and press them in place. Five is good if there's room, but you can get away with four.

30 Now let's add leaves. If you can, use a flat, irregular green pearl (these are "biwa"- style pearls—aren't they yummy!). If you can't find any, use any pearl, stone, or glass bead that will give a nice contrast like this. If they have a hole in the bottom great! Wire 'em up!

33

35

33 You don't need many leaves, and if you keep them around the panda, they will be less likely to be bonked about and broken.

The cuff is fine as is, and you can stop here if you like and bake it, but this last step really adds an unusual look—worth the effort, I think.

But before we do that, you'll need to prebake the cuff. This will set all the sculpture, making the next part much easier. Bake for 20–25 minutes at 275ºF (130ºC).

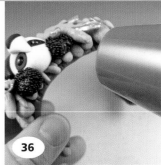

34

34 Once it's cooled down, we're on to the last bit. We're going to use glass micro beads to make the panda's fur really pop! There are several ways to do this, including using glues, but I find that the liquid clay method gives me more control, and more ease in fixing any wayward balls before they are permanently attached in the wrong place. Use a small paintbrush and spread on a layer of liquid clay over the ears. Be careful not to get it on any of the bamboo or white of the panda.

35 Now sprinkle the micro beads all over the liquid clay. Keep sprinkling until all the liquid clay is covered in beads.

36

36 Use a heat gun to set the liquid clay, securing the beads. (If you don't have a heat gun, you can set the liquid clay by baking in the oven for 10–15 minutes at 275ºF (130ºC). Let it cool before continuing each step of the way.

37

Finishing Touches

37 Now move on to the arm. Cover it with liquid clay, then sprinkle beads, then set them with the heat gun or oven. Finally do the eye patches—carefully. You can add liquid clay and beads to build up any areas that are a little patchy (we don't want our panda to be shedding, do we?).

Once the black is done, switch to the white areas. I chose to use clear beads instead of white, because the white were just too distracting—the clear work, dontcha think?

Use tweezers or the tip of a craft knife to nick off any wayward beads that get in the wrong area. Tah dah! Looks bubblicious, huh?!

38 Now give the whole piece a final bake in the oven. Let it cool completely. OK, now the glass micro beads are not going to stick in the liquid clay permanently. You've probably noticed a few starting to wander off already. The best thing to do is to now cover the panda with a clear coating, sandwiching in the beads, which will indeed make them permanently secure. Use a low gloss, such as matte or satin, and coat the entire panda, right over the micro beads—everything except the eyes (they're wired in and fine). Let that dry and then coat it again. Now it's ready for the finishing touches, and then go show that baby off at your next soiree!

- Patina: to really make the bamboo details noticeable, use a medium or light brown acrylic to patina that part of the cuff. Stay away from the panda—any paint there will just look muddy.

- Clear coat—well, you know this part—it's in the steps and it's important!

- Adding clasp (optional)—as mentioned in the Tip on page 59. You can add jump rings to the wire loops (if you added wire loops), then add the clasp to make the cuff more secure.

Winging It
Flying Bird Focal Bead

Size: 2½" to 3" (6.4 to 7.6 cm) long

For this project you will need:

- all the usual sculpting tools
- 28-gauge craft wire for adding bead embellishments
- wire for the stringing channel: 16-gauge or thicker
- embellishment beads: I used round and coin-shaped pearls, aquamarine beads, Peruvian opal beads, garnet (4mm) for the eye
- mica powders: in pearl, blue-green, and russet

Feel like flying? OK, let's make a bird bead! There are so many kinds of birds that the rest of this book could easily be filled with all those feathered friends, but for this project, let's not create a specific breed. Let's make a fantasy bird with a bit of a cockatiel crest, some tail plumage to rival a bird of paradise, and accents of beads and pearls that a peacock would be proud of. Sound like fun?

Clay Recipe

1. White (amount: 1 to 1.5 oz.)
2. Main body color: mix white and pearl in equal amounts. To that add about half as much ecru clay (amount: 1 to 1.5 oz.).
3. Ecru (amount: 0.5 oz.)
4. Gold (amount: 0.5 oz.)
5. Copper and gold, mixed in equal amounts (amount: 0.5 oz.)
6. This is my favorite teal: green pearl and blue pearl, mixed together in equal amounts (amount: 0.5 oz.).
7. To make this lighter version, mix in white a little at a time until you get the shade you like—watch out, a little white goes a long way (amount: 0.5 oz.)!
8. Adding more body color to teal will make an even lighter version (amount: 0.5 oz.).

The first step is to mix the special color blends. The recipes for the colors used in this project are here, but you're not limited to those, of course. What kind of bird are you in the mood for? Soft, subtle, and dignified? Use white, grays, and dusty lavenders. Regal? Go with jewel colors of teal, emerald green, and rich purple. Or get feisty and flamboyant in hot pinks, yellows, and limes!

When you blend the colors for this bird, you will need a bit of clay about the size of a walnut for the main body color and smaller bits in those other accent colors, each about the size of an almond. (Walnuts and almonds? Hmmm, this project is nuts!)

Blend the color for the body so that it is a solid color, or with only a few streaks left in the blend. The smaller bits of accent color will become wings and tail feathers, so you can leave more steaks in for fun and variety.

The bird's head, body, and tail base will all be formed from one piece of clay. It makes for a nice flow to the body, especially if there are a few streaks in your mix—all the lines will flow from head to tail and add to the illusion of motion.

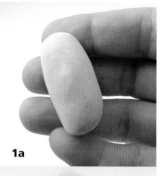
1a

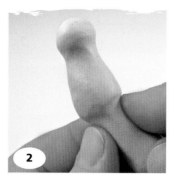
2

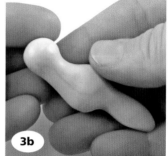
3a

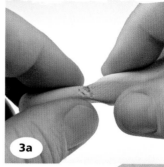
4a

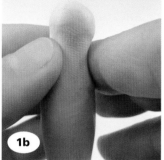
1b

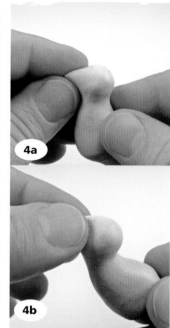

2 Now do the same pinch-and-roll with your fingers to indent the body from the tail. The body should be a little longer than the head.

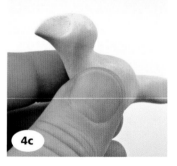
3b

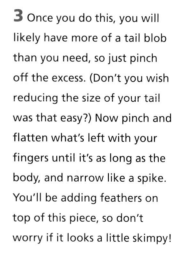

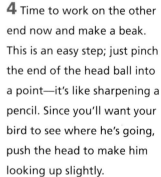
4b

1 Start by taking a piece of clay about the size of your thumb from the main mix and roll it into a smooth ball, making sure there are no surface creases (birds hate to get wrinkly). Roll that into a log. Now, with your fingers, pinch, and roll a neck—an indentation to separate the head from the body.

3 Once you do this, you will likely have more of a tail blob than you need, so just pinch off the excess. (Don't you wish reducing the size of your tail was that easy?) Now pinch and flatten what's left with your fingers until it's as long as the body, and narrow like a spike. You'll be adding feathers on top of this piece, so don't worry if it looks a little skimpy!

4c

4 Time to work on the other end now and make a beak. This is an easy step; just pinch the end of the head ball into a point—it's like sharpening a pencil. Since you'll want your bird to see where he's going, push the head to make him looking up slightly.

5

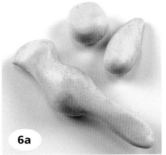

6a

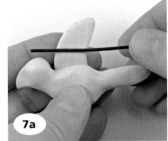

7a

5 Set the piece down and check out the shape—everything look right?

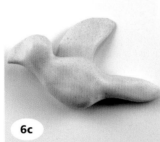

6b

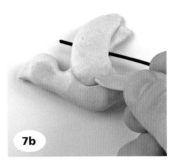

7b

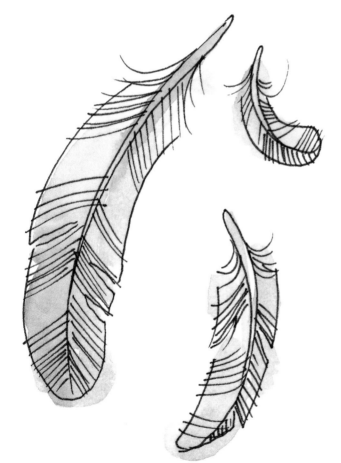

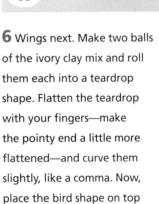

6c

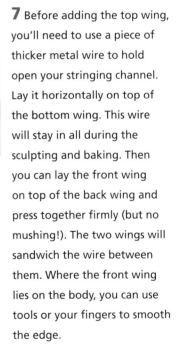

6 Wings next. Make two balls of the ivory clay mix and roll them each into a teardrop shape. Flatten the teardrop with your fingers—make the pointy end a little more flattened—and curve them slightly, like a comma. Now, place the bird shape on top of one of the wings and press slightly to attach the back wing.

7 Before adding the top wing, you'll need to use a piece of thicker metal wire to hold open your stringing channel. Lay it horizontally on top of the bottom wing. This wire will stay in all during the sculpting and baking. Then you can lay the front wing on top of the back wing and press together firmly (but no mushing!). The two wings will sandwich the wire between them. Where the front wing lies on the body, you can use tools or your fingers to smooth the edge.

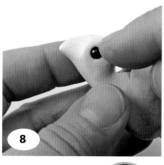

8

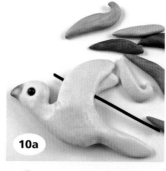

10a

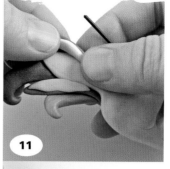

11

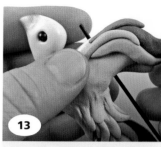

13

9

10b

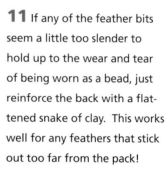

12

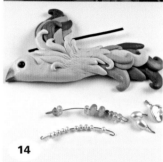

14

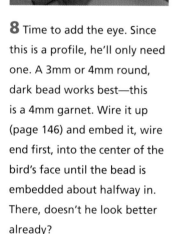

10c

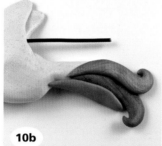

8 Time to add the eye. Since this is a profile, he'll only need one. A 3mm or 4mm round, dark bead works best—this is a 4mm garnet. Wire it up (page 146) and embed it, wire end first, into the center of the bird's face until the bead is embedded about halfway in. There, doesn't he look better already?

9 Since he's getting his face done, let's spruce up the beak while we're in the neighborhood. There are several ways to add color to the beak; the nicest-looking way is to brush mica powder onto the surface of the soft clay (you can also brush on acrylic paint after the piece is baked). Use a soft-haired paintbrush and gently brush the powder on the beak. Blow to remove excess powder (but no sneezing—that's a mess).

10 Now the fun part—adding the feathers! Start by rolling little snakes of clay out of the various colors in your clay blend palette (all those bits of color you mixed up at the beginning). Flatten each slightly with your fingers. Start at the tip of the tail and lay on the feather, pressing firmly but gently to attach. Work your way up the tail, toward the body, overlapping as you go, like roof shingles. Vary the colors that you use, and the sizes and amount of curl as well—birds love variety.

11 If any of the feather bits seem a little too slender to hold up to the wear and tear of being worn as a bead, just reinforce the back with a flattened snake of clay. This works well for any feathers that stick out too far from the pack!

12 As you continue adding overlapping waves of feathers, make them shorter and shorter as you head to the body; the last layer should be the same color as the body. Blend the ends of those feathers into the body with a tool or finger. This will help make it look like the feathers are indeed growing out of the body and not just lying there like a bad toupee. Your bird will thank you for this extra little touch.

13 Feather the wings, in the same way—start at the tips and work toward the body, following the curve of the wings.

14 The well-dressed fantasy bird is wearing pearls this season, so let's add some. Oh, let's add some other fun embellishments, too! Wire up some single beads in the usual way—pearls usually work well for this—and also wire up some strands of beads (page 147). The strands here are Peruvian opals and aquamarine disk-cut beads, but any shape will work (although smaller beads are a bit better than large beads in this situation). Choose any color that matches your bird.

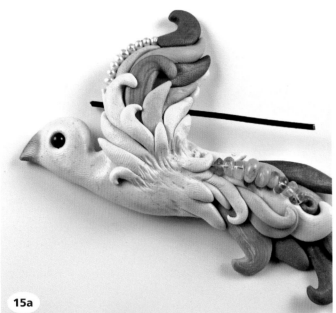

15a

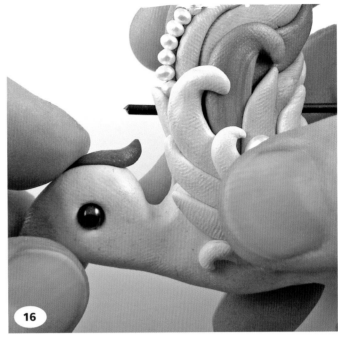

16

16 Hmm, he looks bald. We can't have that, so it's time for a crest. The crest is created in the same way as the wing and tail feathers, only with smaller bits of clay. Start back toward the neck and overlap the bits, moving toward the beak. You'll only need a few and the clay doesn't need to be flattened. Lay one feather on top of the next and don't forget the curls! For strength, you can double up by adding a second row of crest bits behind the first. Make them just a little smaller than the first set, and they shouldn't interfere with the look.

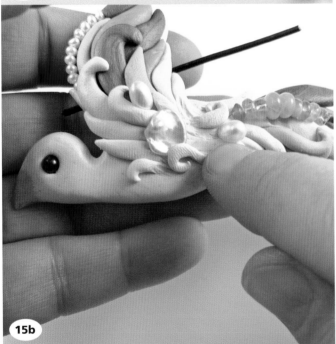

15b

15 Press the individual beads in firmly. Use needle-nose tweezers to embed the wires of the bead strands in place. Push down on the strands to keep them close to the bird's body—it's more stable that way. You can use little balls or curls of clay to cover any exposed wires, too—one of my favorite tricks.

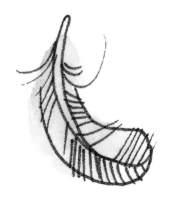

17a

17b

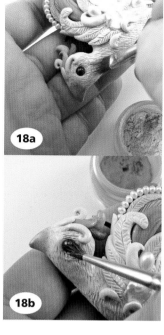

18a

18b

19

17 He's great as he is, but there are a few textural details that can add that final charm. For example, adding some "realistic" lines to the feathers really emphasizes their featheriness! Use a needle tool, or other sculpting tool with a point, and impress a line down the center of a feather—pick one at random to get started. Now press little lines on both sides of that center line—they will all point up toward the base of the feather (where it would be attached to the skin, if this were a real bird). The lines will look like little Vs. Do this to as many or as few feathers as you like.

If you want, you can also press little downy feather strokes in the chest and head area to complete the look.

18 Last, but certainly not least, you can give him an all-over shimmery shine by adding a dust of mica powder on the chest, wing tips, and around the eyes. Pearl white is good for the light-colored body with some blue-green around the eyes and on the wing tips.

All done!

19 Time to bake (follow all the usual guidelines). Remove the stringing wire after the bird is completely cool. Add a patina and clear coating if you choose. (A light brown paint will complement this light-colored body—or you can use a pale teal, if you want to add some extra color.)

Now string him up in a necklace and get ready to fly high on all the compliments you'll receive; or string up a shorter loop of beads to create a hanging loop, and let him fly on a wall as a small sculpture. Either way, what a fine, feathered fellow.

Here are some more bird beads to nudge your creativity!

▶ For stringing this bird, wire pendant loops are inserted into each wing tip in the back. He's adorned with pearls and a sterling silver set faceted citrine, which was once a drop on a necklace. The silver loop on the drop was bent and embedded into the clay to help hold the jewel in place. Pretty slick, huh?

◀ In this fiery fellow, accents of coral and carnelian seemed the logical choice!

◀ The muted grays and earthy lavenders are nicely complemented by amethyst and fluorite bead accents.

▶ This nosey fellow's beak was created by slicing off the tip of his face—don't worry, I used anesthesia, he didn't feel a thing—and adding a nice, big, orange replacement beak.

Prickly on the Outside

Porcupine Mini Sculpture

Size: 2" (5.1 cm) long

For this project you will need:

- a long, pointy tool for poking, not quite as pointy as a needle tool—a knitting needle is perfect, or something similar
- broom straws
- flexible beading wire: gold-colored—medium or heavy weight (0.015" diameter or larger)
- eyes: two lampworked glass eyes preferably, but any round, dark 4mm beads will work
- acrylic paint in a medium brown (raw sienna + burnt umber mixed together make the perfect color) and a flat-tipped brush (a brush used for oil or acrylic painting would be best)
- mica powder (optional): rusty red, like PearlEx 689 Blue Russet, or similar

Have you ever hugged a porcupine? Doesn't this one make you want to? They really do have quite a huggable personality, it's just that exterior that gets in the way! This little sculpture will look nice surveying the area from atop a wooden post, just like his real counterpart, which can often be found up in the trees.

Clay Recipe

1. Body color = ecru + silver + burnt umber—two parts ecru to one part each of the other two colors (amount: 1.5 to 2 oz.)

Mix up your clay color. I went with a lot of ecru in the mix, to match the broom straws we'll be using, but you can adjust the color with more silver, or even add a touch of black for a deeper gray. Mix the colors thoroughly, there's no need to leave any streaks of unblended color, really.

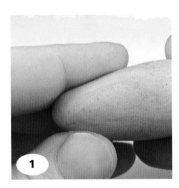

1 Make a ball out of the clay about the size of an avocado pit. Roll that into a narrow egg shape—tapered narrower at one end than the other.

2 The shape is really easy; just need to pinch a bit of a snout at the narrower end. Pinch gently, moving all around the clay so that the tapering is even (no squish marks!). You'll want it to look like he has a forehead that slopes to a snout, so press with your thumb to make that curve.

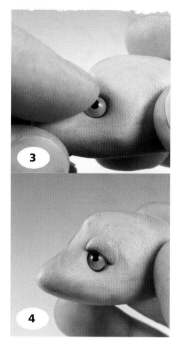

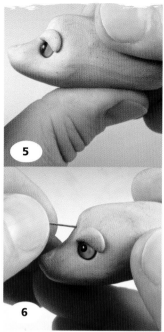

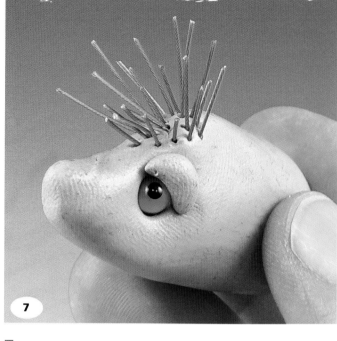

3 Now add eyes. Just press into place, making sure they are lined up and even on both sides. Press them in so that they are almost even with the surface of the clay.

4 He's sleepy (don't ask me how I know, I just do), so he needs some slightly droopy eyelids. Just roll two little balls of clay of the same body color into rice-shaped bits. Curve them a bit on the tip of your finger. Now press them in place above the eye. Make sure they are slightly back of center, not forward, or you'll have a grouchy porcupine (unless of course you want a grouchy porcupine, in which case, go right ahead!). Obviously, give him eyelids on both eyes.

5 Now flatten the bottom a bit so he can stand up well. Just press him against the work surface, or use your finger to flatten a little.

6 The hair on his forehead area will be shorter and sticking forward a bit (he's using a new gel and it really gives that "stand up and take notice" look). Snip bits of beading wire (coated flexible steel cable, used for necklace stringing) into pieces about ½" (1.3 cm) or so long. Now just press them into the clay with fingers or pliers.

7 Keep on poking them in there until he has a spiky 'do!

Now for the rest of the pokeys all over the body. I chose to make his quills out of broom straws because they are easy to find, cheap, and quite flexible, so they resist snapping even after baking. Of course you could use other things—wire, nails (use the finish nails with the tiny heads, and stick them in with the pointy side out), bamboo skewers or toothpicks (although they may have a tendency to crack during baking), or even actual porcupine quills (they are available!).

I like using the broom straws—they have that wild look that all the young porcupines are going for this season. I recommend using the natural broom straws in the golden color (not the green) if you can find them. If you can't, just snip some off of your neighbor's broom when she isn't looking! (Kidding!)

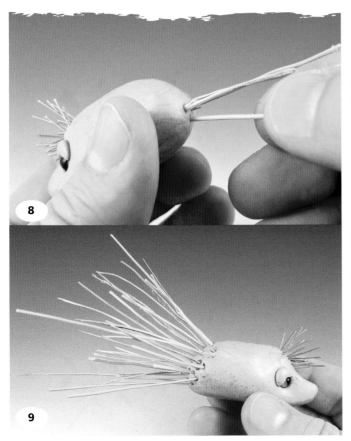

8

10a

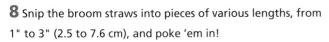

9

10b

8 Snip the broom straws into pieces of various lengths, from 1" to 3" (2.5 to 7.6 cm), and poke 'em in!

9 Keep poking!

10 Make all the straws angle back, as if he's facing the wind. Work from the back, toward the face. As you get to the face, you can use shorter and shorter straws.

Finally, add a few long pieces of the beading wire in the back and a few pieces of short straws in the forehead area, just to make sure all the bits look like they belong together.

11

12

13

11 Now for this dude not to look like someone just poked a bunch of straw bits into a piece of clay (who could possibly think that?), there are two little tricks we're going to do. The first is now, before baking, and the other is after baking. Take a long, pointy tool, such as a skewer or a knitting needle, and poke the whole surface of his body, in between all the straws and cables except for his face, which would look like he has the chicken pox. (Or is it the porky pox?).

12 The only hint of facial features you need to give him is a little definition in the nose area. You can make a full face with nose and cheeks and mouth (best to do that before all the straws get poked in, of course), but it's not really necessary—he looks nice just as is, I think.

OK, he's done, but hmmmm … he needs something.

13 How about just a little glow of powder on his nose. Use a soft brush and just swipe right on the tip. Perfecto.

OK, the sculpting's done— go bake him!

▶ It's a little known fact of nature that the porcupine uses up to three gallons of hair gel a year to get his spikes to stand up like that.

14 Once he's all the way cool, time for that last little trick I mentioned. We're going to add some paint to the body, and by happy accident to the base of the straws as well, which will bring the whole thing together. Use a medium brown acrylic paint, and with your brush dab the paint onto the body. You'll have to keep lifting the brush up and out, and repositioning it down in a new spot between the straws, but if you don't have too much paint on the brush, you should be able to coat the surface of the porcupine body without too much paint getting onto the ends of the straws. (And if it does, no biggie—just wipe it off with a damp sponge.) Remember this isn't adding a patina, you're not going to wipe it off. You're just adding a layer of color to take away his nakedness.

15 Let him dry and then perch him on a nice wooden lookout post.

Finishing Touches

- Patina just around the eyes: use the same color acrylic as for the body coverage.
- No clear coating needed.

TIP: If the broom straws ever get dried out and seem brittle, set him upside down in a bowl of warm water for an hour or so—the straws will soak up the water and become supple again, thereby resisting any disappointing snaps!

Lounge Lizard
Gecko Sculpture

Size: 5" (12.7 cm)

For this project you will need:

- all the usual sculpting tools
- cutting blade
- wire cutters and pliers
- eyes: two round, dark beads (I used 10mm Venetian glass—dark blue with silver foil core, which makes a nice inner glow just right for eyes!)
- glass micro beads (also called holeless glass beads): in two colors (I used raspberry and purple)
- glue (any that will accommodate heat, and adhere to glass and plastic)
- mica powder (optional): in a matching color (I used PearlEx 654 Super Russet + 688 Misty Lavender)

If you've played with clay for any length of time, you've probably accumulated a small (or large) wad of scrap clay—bits and pieces from projects, cane ends, color blends that didn't work out well—you know, scraps. What to do with them? You can't throw them out, it's good polymer clay after all! But it's all messy ... Well, here's the perfect project for that wad—a gecko! Geckos naturally come in all kind of colors, so whatever you have will be just right!

Once he's finished, this large lizard can live among your houseplants or scamper up a wall in the bathroom—a tribute to the idea that even scraps can be beautiful!

1

Clay Recipe

1. Scrap clay! Any color you have lying around. (I used a wad with white, pearl, ecru, pinks, and blues in it.) (amount: 3 to 4 oz.)

1

2

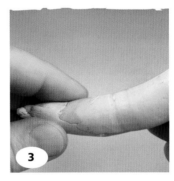

3

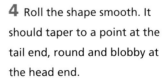

5

1 First of all, take that wad and run it through the pasta machine a couple times to see what color it will become. (Treat it like a Lookit blend [page 18] in the way that you run it through, fold it, and run it through again.) Stop when you have a nice blend, like this.

2 Now roll it up to keep the fun colors on the outside. Make sure you roll it nice and tight.

3 Shape the roll into a long teardrop shape. There will probably be more than you need, so pinch it off and set it aside to use for legs later.

4 Roll the shape smooth. It should taper to a point at the tail end, round and blobby at the head end.

5 Now form a neck by rolling and squeezing about 1" (2.5 cm) down from the blobby end.

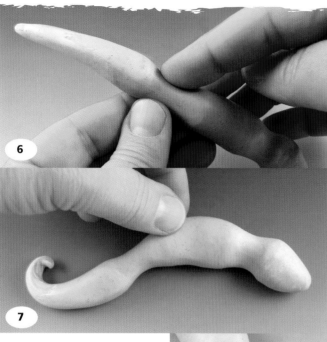

6

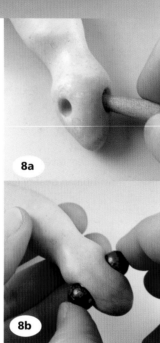

7

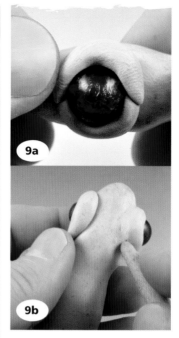

9a

9b

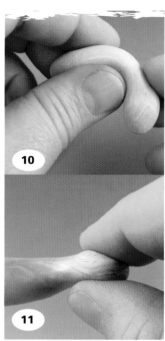

10

11

8a

8b

6 Make a distinction between the body and start of the tail by doing the same pinching and rolling trick.

7 Curve his body in a gecko-like kind of way—a nice S curve!

8 Geckos have big ol' eyes—it's part of their charm. Wire up some large, round beads (check the Resources pages for a source on these cool Venetian glass ones). Create a hole on each side of the head for the eye beads to press into first. For beads this big, just pressing them in without a guiding hole can get a little messy. Notice that the holes are almost in the center of each side of the face—not up high on the head (again, it's all about the cuteness!).

Press the eye beads in.

9 He'll look silly with the bulgy ol' eyes just sticking out, so add a snake of clay above and below the beads, and blend that clay into the head. Doesn't that look better!

10 Time for legs. From the extra clay you have, roll out four logs of clay. Pick up one (this will be a front leg) and shape it so that it has a bit of a blobby end (the toes will be made from this). Bend it in what will pass as an elbow for this dude.

11 Flatten the blob a little.

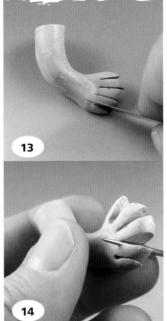

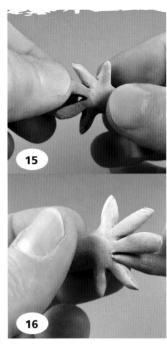

12 The back leg begins the same, but make a nice sharp bend for the ankle, then a bend for the knee. Slice the ends off of the limbs, so when it's time they will smooth onto the body really easily. This is how the legs should look. Make the other side limbs while you're at it.

13 Making the toes takes a little patience, but I know you can do it. He needs five toes. Sometimes you can get away with less in a stylized version of a creature, but five really work for a gecko; gives him that almost-human quality (in a good way, of course). Start by slicing four slices to make five fairly equal sections.

14 Now use your needle tool to press between each cut and separate the toes.

15 Now gently pinch and roll each section into toes. Start on the outer toes and work in. Don't pull or they'll get too long and skinny. Just roll them in your fingertips and they'll shape up nicely.

16 Use a dowel tool next, to smooth the space between the toes a little more. Usually this is all you need to do to finish up the toe sections.

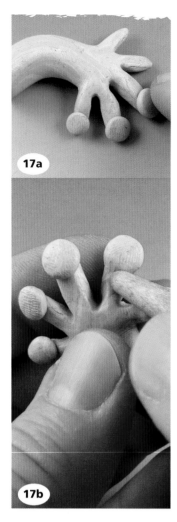

17a

17b

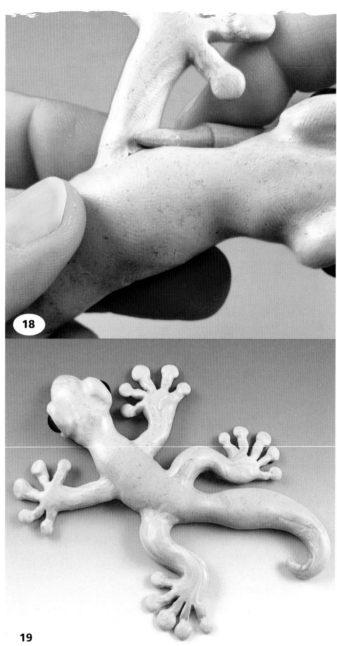

18

19

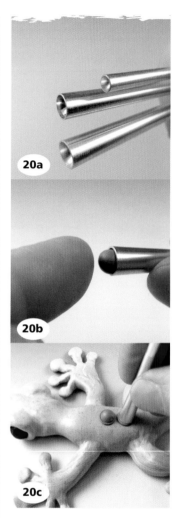

20a

20b

20c

17 Now to make them cute! Roll out little balls of clay and press a ball onto the tip of each toe. Smooth each ball onto the toe so that it looks like a nice gecko toe and not a strange lollipop.

Wasn't that fun? Good, because you have to do it to every toe on all four legs. Whew, you better go fortify yourself with a little chocolate snack first.

18 OK, well done! Now attach each leg by pressing it firmly into place and smoothing the clay from the limb onto the body with a tool. To give yourself a little more clay to smooth with, it helps to flare the clay at the attaching end of the limbs.

19 Once the legs are in position, make sure his shape is good—legs forward and back, that body curved still, tail curled—you know, lizardy!

20 I think a row of dots down his back would be cool. Roll out balls of clay and press them into place. Or use one of these cool cupped tools from Sculpey. Stick the ball into the cup and press it on his back— little scoops of ice cream! Yum!

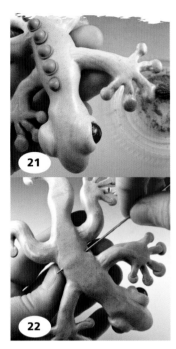
21

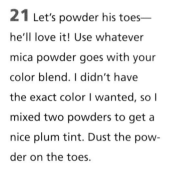
22

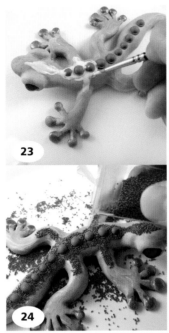
23

24

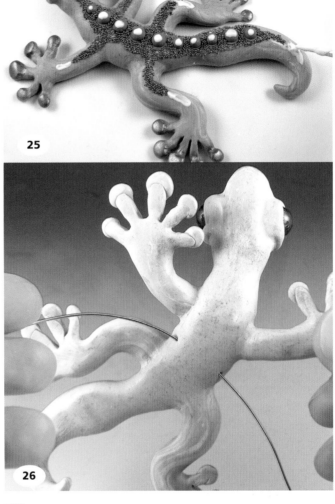
25

26

21 Let's powder his toes—he'll love it! Use whatever mica powder goes with your color blend. I didn't have the exact color I wanted, so I mixed two powders to get a nice plum tint. Dust the powder on the toes.

22 If you want to have the option of attaching this guy to a basket or plant stem, poke him in the belly with a needle tool. Then you can slip a wire or string through there later.

Bake him completely. Don't forget to prop his head up with paper or tissue!

The last fun touch will be adding the sprinkles of glass micro beads to his back. We used liquid clay to adhere these beads onto the panda, but for this guy, let's use glue instead, so you don't have to coat over the balls with a clear coating if you don't want to.

23 Use a paintbrush to paint a thick layer of glue all around the dots from forehead to tail. I used Weldbond glue, which works reasonably well as long as the beads aren't going to be getting a lot of handling (so don't rub his back for luck, OK?).

24 Pour on the micro beads!

25 If you want to do a little two-tone fun, add some more glue to the outer edges of the bead zone, and dump on another color. (I put some glue in the center of the blue dots on his back, so they could sparkle, too.)

26 Let the glue dry, shake off any excess micro beads, and he's ready to frolic! Add the wire to his belly if you want to attach him to a basket or plant.

Wet and Wild

Water and Ocean Creatures and Designs

Tide Pool Vessel, *page 94*

Water, water everywhere—ponds and lakes and oceans! All of it teeming with life, all that life just waiting to become a little polymer clay project. Yup, that's the meaning of life—polymer clay project potential (and you thought it was more complicated and deep, huh?).

Sea Turtle Sculpture, *page 88*

Ocean Sunset Wall Piece, *page 100*

As with everything else we've done so far, stylizing is the name of the game! Water lends itself to that, of course. It can be calm and mesmerizing, or tempestuous—the home of the lowly pond scum, or playpen of the Loch Ness monster. So we'll have a lot to inspire us in this chapter!

Ammonite Fossil Pin, *page 106*

Picture Frame, *page 112*

Ready to slip-slide into this next chapter? **Splash!**

Dot's Nice
Sea Turtle Sculpture

Size: 3" (7.6 cm)

For this project you will need:

- all the usual sculpting tools
- cutting blade
- wire cutters and pliers
- eyes: two round, dark 4mm beads
- beads for the turtle's shell: a round, flat bead with a hole drilled through lengthwise is best (these are jasper)

Ready to make a big splash with wet and wild projects? This little sea turtle is just the place to start—he's wild, all right (you should hear the parties he throws!) and he's wet (well, duh, he's a turtle).

This swell fellow also sports a lovely jasper-coated shell (it's what all the well-dressed turtles are wearing this season).

Clay Recipe

1. Dark green for accents = ecru + fluorescent green + sea green + burnt umber + ultramarine blue (mostly the greens, with just little smidgens of the other colors) (amount: 1 to 1.5 oz.)

2. Medium green for the shell = ecru + fluorescent green (equal parts) + just a bit of gold (amount: 1 to 1.5 oz.)

3. Lighter green for the body = ecru + fluorescent green (three parts ecru to one part fluorescent green) (amount: 1 to 1.5 oz.)

1 We'll start with the bottom shell, which will support all the turtle bits—head, flippers, and tail. From the medium-color clay, roll out a small oval and flatten it in your hands.

2 Set that aside and use the lightest green clay to roll a log of clay. This will be his head, so make sure one end is especially smooth and rounded (this will be his snout end).

3 To create eye sockets, and give the face a bit of definition, hold that rounded end with thumb and forefinger and squeeze to make noticeable indentations. If you squeeze too hard the clay will squinch up in the middle. That's OK, though, just press it back down.

4 Sea turtles have a bit of a beak, so just pinch the lower portion of his face to create a downward-turning point.

5 Now wire up the two dark, round beads for the eyes and press them into the centers of the eye sockets.

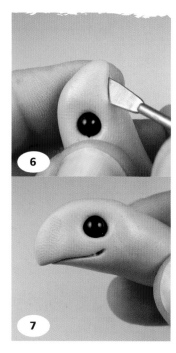

6

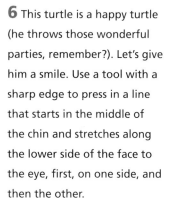

7

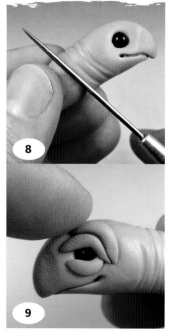

8

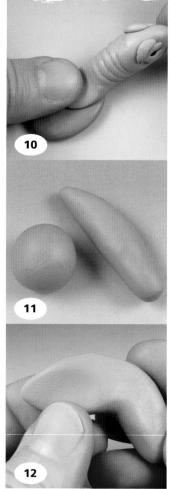

9

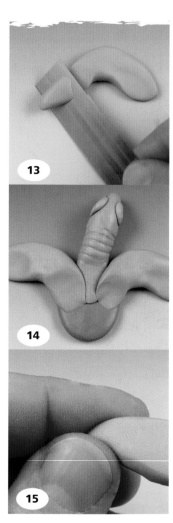

10

11

12

13

14

15

6 This turtle is a happy turtle (he throws those wonderful parties, remember?). Let's give him a smile. Use a tool with a sharp edge to press in a line that starts in the middle of the chin and stretches along the lower side of the face to the eye, first, on one side, and then the other.

7 End the line in a slight upturn—now there's a happy turtle!

8 If you've looked at any turtles lately, you'll have noticed that they have wrinkles on their necks. (They do, I've checked!) So, let's add some to this guy with a needle tool. Don't scratch them in, just roll them in with the edge of the tool.

9 Next he'll get some detailing around his eyes. Roll out two small, rice-shaped bits from the same clay color as the face. Bend each into an arc and press into place—one under the eye bead, and one over the eye bead. He's a mellow dude, so don't give him angry eyes by placing the top eyelid too far forward. Make and press in another eyelid over the top one. Turtles have wrinkly eyelids.

Do the other eye the same way, of course.

10 Now the head is done. Press it onto the shell bottom that you set aside earlier. Just push the bottom of the neck onto the top of that oval.

11 OK, on to the flippers— front ones first. Roll out two balls of the same color clay as the head. Shape them into teardrops.

12 Bend the flippers into curves and flatten them with your fingers. This will create the perfect paddlelike shapes.

13 Get rid of some of the excess clay at the armpit end of the flippers by slicing them at an angle.

14 Now press the flippers onto the shell bottom, right beside the turtle's neck. It looks best, I think, to angle them forward a little bit. (He has places to go, people to see.)

15 Back flippers are shorter and rounder—they are the rudders, so they don't have to do much paddling. Roll out the shape, flatten, and press into place on the bottom shell.

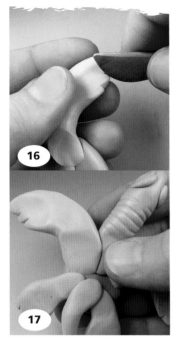

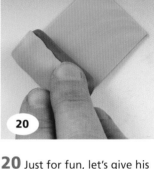

16 He needs toes, don't you think? Me, too. Just press some indentations into the clay with the edge of a sculpting tool. Press the tool into the edge of the clay and then roll it up onto the surface just a little ways to create a nice wedge shape. Do this to both front and back flippers.

17 Add a tail by rolling out a snake of clay and pressing it on between the back flippers.

18 Well, now all the turtley bits are on the bottom shell and he's ready for his top shell. Roll some of the medium green clay into an oval shape and flatten it slightly. Continue to flatten just the outside edges by gently pinching all around to make a slightly squished half-dome. Now use your thumb to press an indentation into one end of the oval (this is where the neck will poke out) and pinch the opposite end into a tapered point (this is where the tail will poke out).

19 Place this top shell gently over the bottom shell with all the attached turtley bits. If it's too small, you can pull, squeeze, and press to widen the shape to fit. If it's too big, it's usually easiest to roll the clay back up into a ball, pinch off some clay so the ball is smaller, and remake the shape.

Once the top shell is in position, attach it by pressing along the sides.

20 Just for fun, let's give his head, flippers, and tail some extra pizzazz! So, are you ready to make the world's simplest cane?

Roll out a cylinder of the darker green clay about as thick as your finger. Slice the ends straight off. Now use either your light green or your medium green clay and roll a sheet through the pasta machine's thickest setting. Trim the sheet so that it is the same width as the cylinder. Now roll it up! Press tightly as you roll.

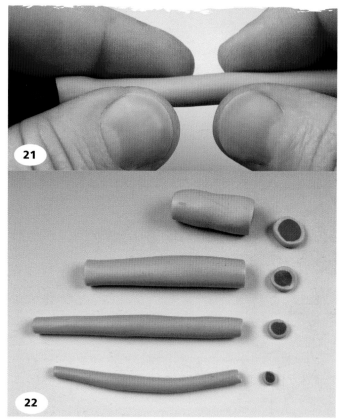

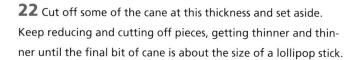

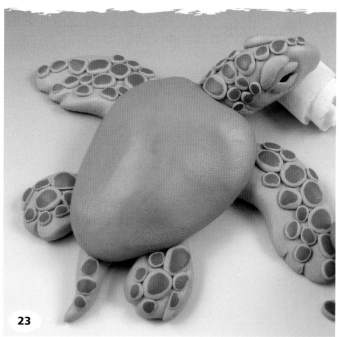

23 With your blade, cut off thin slices (about as thick as a dime, or thinner) from each of the canes and start laying them on the turtle's body—the biggest ones in the middle of his flippers and down the center of his neck, adding smaller and smaller bits around those until as much of the surface of his body is covered as possible. Don't forget those dots down his tail!

21 Reduce the cane by squeezing, pulling, and rolling (remember all the little tricks we chatted about in the beginning of the book about making canes) until the cylinder is thin—a little thinner than a pencil.

22 Cut off some of the cane at this thickness and set aside. Keep reducing and cutting off pieces, getting thinner and thinner until the final bit of cane is about the size of a lollipop stick.

25

27

24 Now let's jazz up his back. Roll out small balls of the dark green clay and press them flat with your fingers (like little pancakes!). Start with one in the center of his back and then surround it with a circle of others.

25 Wire up some beads (I used flat, round jasper beads) and press them into the circles of clay.

26 Add more flattened balls of dark green clay to make the shell look just right!

27 Make any final adjustments to the angle of his head and the curve of his flippers, because he's ready to bake. Oh, and roll up a strip of paper to prop his head up (he <u>has</u> had a long night partying), otherwise the neck could crack during baking. (Turtles hate it when their necks crack, you know.) Bake as usual.

Now call all his friends for a housewarming party at his new beachfront property!

Finishing Touches

- Patina with burnt sienna or burnt umber, if you wish.
- No need to add any clear coating!

Little Water World
Tide Pool Vessel

Size: 8" (20.3 cm) wide

For this project you will need:

- all the usual sculpting tools
- cutting blade
- rock chips
- liquid clay
- clear glass chips
- shells
- sea urchin spines (or dagger beads)
- pearls, lampwork glass beads, other embellishment beads
- 28-gauge craft wire for attaching beads
- head pins
- shallow glass bowl
- EnviroTex Lite or similar product
- mica powder (optional): PearlEx 681 Duo Blue-Green
- two 3mm or 4mm dark, round beads for fish eyes
- flexible mesh (optional) for scale texture

Well, I'm still in an oceany mood, aren't you? So let's make a little ocean world that you can hold in the palm of your hands.

A shallow glass bowl works best because you can leave a little porthole open in the bottom. Then set your ocean world over a picture of a mermaid or other sea creature. You could use a metal or ceramic bowl instead, just don't leave the opening on the bottom.

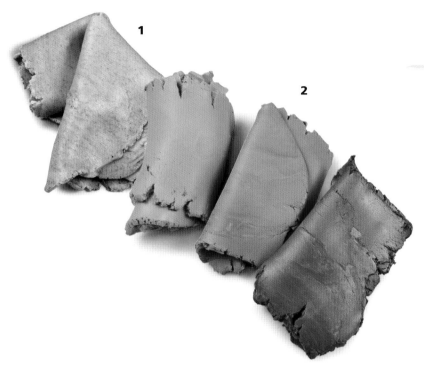

1

2

Clay Recipe

1. Sandy mix for covering the bowl = pearl + ecru + Cernit quartz (two parts pearl to one part each of the others) + just a smidgen of burnt umber (amount: 6 to 8 oz.)

2. Sea urchins and starfish: equal parts orange + copper + gold = the darkest of the colors; to make the lighter variations, cut the mix into thirds and set one third aside. To the next third, add an equal amount of ecru and mix, set aside. To the final third, add two parts ecru and mix thoroughly. (amount: 2 oz. of each blend)

1 Cover the bowl with the sandy clay mix. You'll need quite a bit of it, if your bowl is large, like this one. You can use a smaller bowl, of course. Roll the sandy clay through the pasta machine at a middle setting so the clay is thin enough to go a long way and cover nicely, but not so thin that it rips too easily. Just press it firmly in place; it'll stay.

Don't expect to cover it all with one sheet! A patchwork quilt effect is fine. Leave an irregular hole showing (match up the back-of-the-bowl clay with the hole, too).

2 Once the clay is in place, roughly smooth all the seams with tool and fingers.

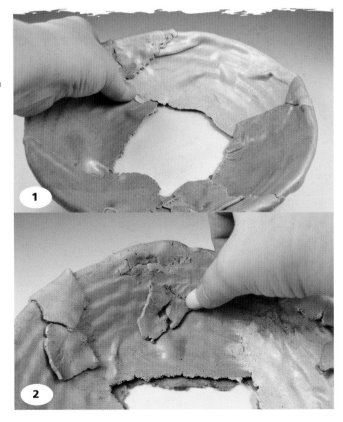

1

2

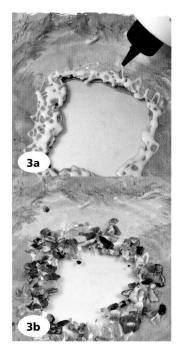

3a

3b

4a

4b

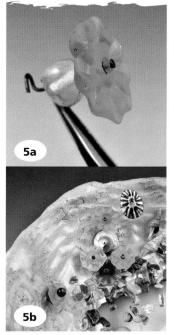

5a

5b

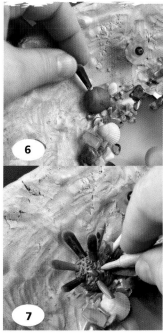

6

7

3 Just for fun, let's put a scattering of rock chips on the bottom of the bowl, all around the opening. To help the rocks stay in place while we add other stuff, zigzag some liquid clay all around the edges of the clay before adding the chips.

4 For that realistic ocean touch, nothing can beat a few real shells here and there. To help them stay put, fill up their holes with liquid clay and then press them into place. The liquid clay will harden inside during baking to connect shell to clay.

5 All kinds of beads can be added to the clay in the bottom of the bowl to make it a full, vibrant community! These are some wonderful flat riffle lampwork glass beads that look nautically magnificent—especially when the "water" gets added. Put a glass seed bead on a headpin first, then slide on the glass bead, trim, and bend the headpin. Make several of these, and add a larger glass bead to some for height variety, if you want. Press them firmly into the sides. I find it helpful to add a little ball of sand-colored clay first to give the wire enough clay to press into.

6 Sea urchin time! Yay! Start with a ball of clay—this deep rust color mix will go great with the sea urchin spine beads. Press the ball into the bowl wherever. Next press the sea urchin spines directly into the clay. (You can get sea urchin spine beads from many bead sellers.) Wire them in or not, since these guys will be under water and the spines have a little knob on the end that will keep them from coming out and floating away while the "water" resin sets.

7 Jam in as many spines as will fit and radiate them out like a fireworks burst. Once they are in place, poke the visible clay all over with little dimples to make a nice pattern.

▼ Tidepools are wonderful! If you've ever been to a seaside with tide pools, it really is like exploring little worlds with their own communities and architecture. In thinking about it, these doodles emerged—lots of jars, glasses, and containers filled with little worlds!

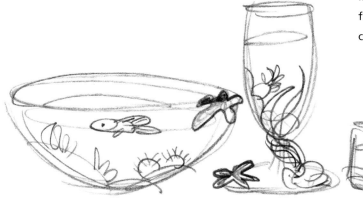

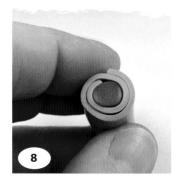

8

9

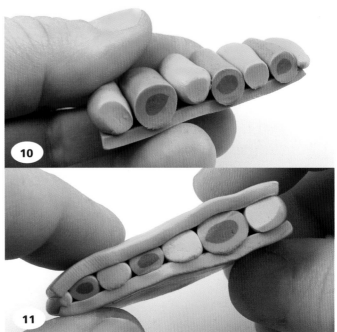

10

11

Make as many sea urchins for this little world as you want, but remember they are noisy neighbors.

What ocean bowl community would be complete without the strong presence of a starfish? To make him, let's make another simple cane! Aw, c'mon, you'll like it, I promise!

8 We'll use all three of the rusty color clays. Take the darkest and roll out a nice log, about as thick as a crayon, and about as long. Take the medium color and run it through the pasta machine to make a sheet. Place the log on the sheet and trim it so that it is as wide as the log is long. Now wrap up the log in the sheet—twice around at least.

9 That's your cane. Honest. Just as easy as the turtle one, huh? Actually, it's pretty much the exact same one as the turtle. Now reduce it to press the clays tight together and to make it thinner and longer. We're going to use several different widths of this same cane, so as you reduce this, keep one side wide and keep tapering the other so that it is half as thick.

10 Chop that cane up into three equal lengths—small, medium, and large. Assemble these cane chunks into a starfish arm cane by using the lightest of the clays and rolling out a sheet. Cut it as wide as the cane chunks are long. With the leftovers, roll out snakes of clay that mimic the cane chunks in width—like twins for each piece. Make one more snake, thinner than the rest. Now lay them in line on the clay sheet, alternating canes and logs, with the thin one at the end. Yup, just like that.

11 All that's left to do is lay another sheet of light-colored clay on top of this sandwich! Once the top sheet is on, press this cane together firmly to remove the air bubbles and gaps (you can squish it together to make it a bit fatter; this helps!). And there you have a starfish arm cane.

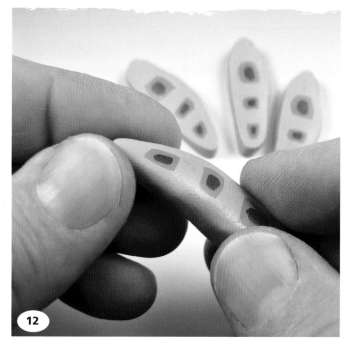

12

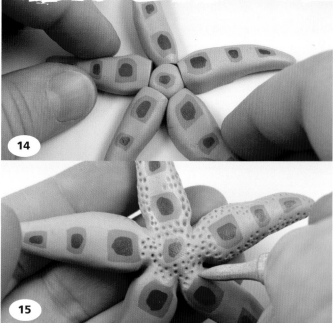

14

15

12 To make the actual starfish out of this, you'll need to get six slices out of this cane! Each slice should be about ¼" (6 mm) thick if possible. If it doesn't look as if you will be able to get that out of the cane, keep squishing it fatter and longer until it's thick enough.

You will be slicing along the length to expose all the little dots on the inside. So, cut the six slices and take five of them to shape into the arms. (Ha! I bet you thought I messed up and forgot that starfish only have five arms and not six! Hee hee, gotcha! Just set the last arm slice aside for the moment.)

To make them into arms, use your fingers to press along the top edges to soften the cut. Pinch the end that has the smallest dot into a tapered point—not too pointy; rounded is best. Do this with all five arms.

13 Now take that sixth arm and slice it so that you have just the largest dot surrounded by the light clay. Form that into a circular shape by pressing the edges until it's a circle.

14 Put the circle in the middle and position the arms all around. Press them together firmly. Use a tool to smooth the clay between the joins so that it looks all one piece. You'll find it helpful to pick it up and smooth in between the arms too. Don't worry about the back; it won't be visible.

15 For a nice look, add dimples—I poked them in all around the outer edges of the legs and a bit in the middle, and left the dot pattern part undimpled. Doesn't he look cute? Sorry, doesn't *she* look cute?!

▶ Use an image, like this mermaid, to slip under the open glass at the bottom of the bowl. You'll be able to glimpse her through the water of the tidepool.

16

16 Press her onto her new home.

Now go bake it! Before we can add the "water," it must be baked thoroughly. Once it's cool, you should add a patina (can't do it once the resin is in the way).

When the patina is finished and everything is dry, we can add the "water." This will be done in stages so the resin can dry for each layer. This also allows us to add some fun bits between the layers.

Mix up the EnviroTex Lite (or similar product) **exactly** according to the instructions. The instructions are simple and clear, so take a moment to read them. It's important that the mix is exactly half and half, and that it's blended together thoroughly for several minutes. If you do those simple things, it works brilliantly!!

17

Only mix up what you're going to use—this polymer compound resin uses a chemical reaction to set, and once it starts, it doesn't wait. You'll need enough to fill the bowl about a third of the way full.

17 I find it best to lay down a piece of foil first (any wayward drips will fall on the foil) and have a cardboard box handy to put over it while it dries to keep the dust off but allow airflow. Pour it in.

18

18 Let it dry according to the instructions. It looks good just like this, doesn't it?

You could stop here, or you could make a friendly fish to frolick around in the middle! To do that, head to my website, www.cforiginals.com, for the free instructions. (Wasn't that a clever way to get you to visit my site?)

Another Day in Paradise

Ocean Sunset Wall Piece

Size: 4½" tall × 3" wide (11.4 × 7.6 cm)

For this project you will need:

- all the usual sculpting tools
- cutting blade
- liquid clay
- embossing powder: any sandy color (I used Jim Holtz brand Distress Powder in Brushed Corduroy color)
- glass leaf-shaped beads (with hole at one end)
- metal mesh ribbon in an ocean color
- flexible plastic screen mesh (get at any hardware store)
- acrylic paint: yellow, blue, white, and pinkish red
- paintbrush
- (optional) metal charms, buttons, or studs (I used a tiny starfish, and a circle shape for the sun)

If you've ever stood on the beach on a tropical island and watched the sunset, you know it's a magical thing. Sunsets are magical anywhere, of course, but there's something about a tropical sunset that makes you feel like you're in paradise. This little wall piece will let you go there in your mind, anyway.

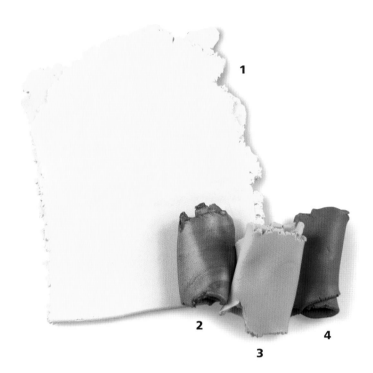

Clay Recipe

1. Background color = equal amounts white + pearl + just a bit of ecru to make an ivory color (amount: 0.5 to 1 oz.)
2. Palm tree bark color = equal amounts gold + copper (amount: 0.5 oz.)
3. Sand = ecru (amount: 0.5 oz.)
4. Leaves and inner tree = any green (this is green pearl + ecru) (amount: 0.5 oz.)

Start by running the ivory clay through the pasta machine at the widest setting to make a background piece about 3" x 4" (7.6 x 10.2 cm). To get the sunset coloring, we could do a Skinner blend, but painting it on will allow us to stretch the clay and create a few crackles that make it feel like clouds in the evening sky.

1 Mix your paint colors by first blopping out a bit of color and using a soft brush to start blending—you'll need a soft blue (white + blue), a pale yellow (white + yellow), and a salmony red (pinkish-red + pale yellow).

2 Now paint these colors in stripes on the surface of the clay. Acrylic paint dries quickly but you shouldn't use much if any water, as it will make the paint bead up on the surface of the clay instead of covering smoothly. Layer the blue on the top, then the yellow (more white between these will keep the blend from getting too green), then the salmony-red. Keep blending until the color looks nice and sunsety!

Set it aside to dry (and go wash out the brush!).

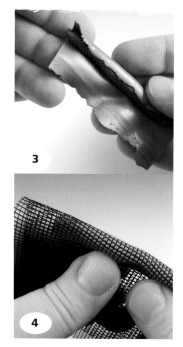

3

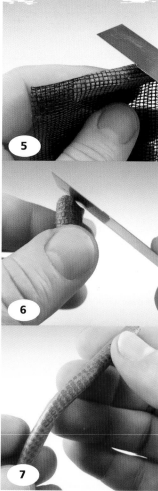

4

5

6

7

8

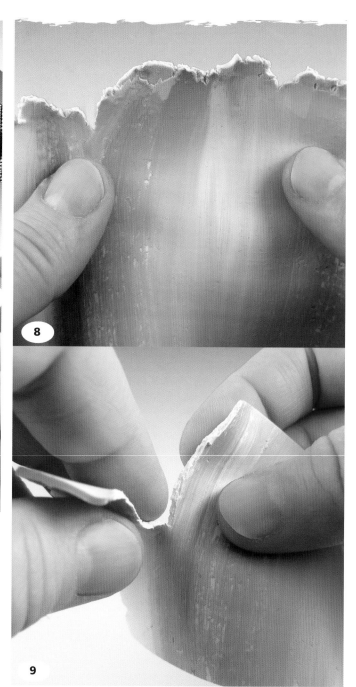

9

3 To make the palm tree, we're going to have a little fun. Roll a log of green clay about as thick as a pencil. Now run the copper-gold mix through the pasta machine at a very, very thin setting—as thin as you can go and still be able to handle the clay. Cut the thin clay into a sheet about as wide as the green log is long. Wrap the copper-gold clay around the green one time and trim away the excess. Gently roll it to make sure the two layers are joined together.

4 Pick up this log and place it in the center of the flexible plastic screen. Fold the screen over it and push so that the clay has squished out in all the little squares.

5 Use a very sharp cutting blade to slice away the coppery clay, exposing little squares of the underlayer of green. Be careful not to slice the screen, if you can.

6 Once you've cut away all you can, gently unwrap the clay from the screen. Cut away any additional bits of copper that you need to to be able to see the pattern.

7 Roll the log on a flat surface to smooth away the jagged bumps (if you like them, don't roll them away). Tah-dah! It's a palm tree trunk. Make another one!

8 Set the trunks aside for a minute and pick up the sunset sheet. It should be dry by now. Give it a nice tug to stretch in some cracks.

9 Cut the sides straight, but rip off the top for a rough edge that will go better with the stretch clouds. (Clay rips better when it's cool, so if it's a hot day in your craft area, pop the clay in the refrigerator for five minutes.) Set that aside for a bit and let's play in the sand.

10

10 Roll the ecru clay through the pasta machine at a medium thickness. Now cover the surface with embossing powder— instant sand! You may wonder why we don't just use real sand. Real sand won't stick, but embossing powder melts on in the oven. (Oh, that will be on the quiz later, so make a note of it.) Set that aside.

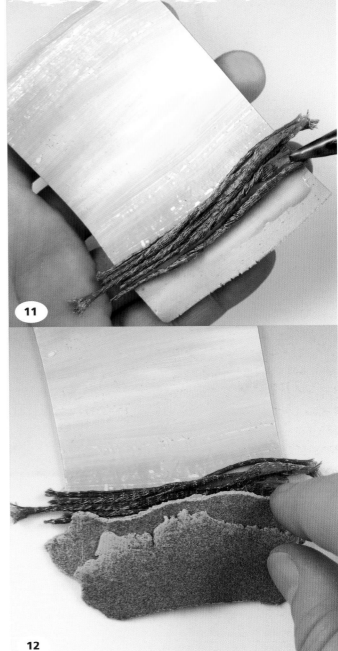

11

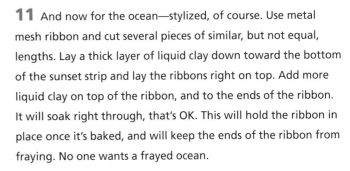

12

11 And now for the ocean—stylized, of course. Use metal mesh ribbon and cut several pieces of similar, but not equal, lengths. Lay a thick layer of liquid clay down toward the bottom of the sunset strip and lay the ribbons right on top. Add more liquid clay on top of the ribbon, and to the ends of the ribbon. It will soak right through, that's OK. This will hold the ribbon in place once it's baked, and will keep the ends of the ribbon from fraying. No one wants a frayed ocean.

12 Take the sandy clay and rip it into strips. Lay several over the bottom of the piece right up to (and a little on top of) the ocean ribbon.

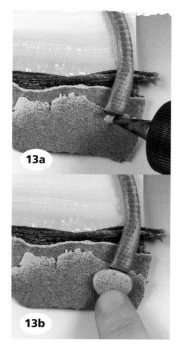

13a

13b

14

15

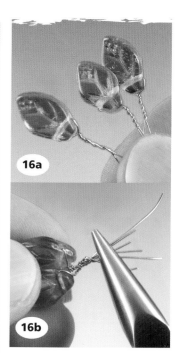

16a

16b

13 Add a thin layer of liquid clay to the back of the palm tree trunk and press it gently into place. Add a little blob of liquid clay right under the palm's base and press a little ball of ecru clay in place. (In case you were wondering, the liquid clay makes sure the clays adhere to all these covered surfaces.) Now lay another layer of sand on top of the ball to cover the trunk of the tree. See how the ball holds the sandy clay up to the same level as the tree. Clever, huh?

16 Wire up a handful of the glass leaf beads and group most in clumps of three with their end wires twisted together.

14 Add the metal starfish (or whatever other cool oceany bit you have!).

Oops, forgot to sneak that second palm tree trunk in there—do it now!

15 Make a leafy base for the glass leaves by rolling out rice-shaped bits of green clay and flattening them. Press them in place at the top of the trees in a fanned-out shape.

17 Press the clumps into the green clay leaf shapes. Press in as many three-leaf clumps as will fit and fill in any gaps with individually wired leaf beads. Isn't that cool! Don't you just want to stretch out under those leaves and nap in the shade? (You'd have to be really small.)

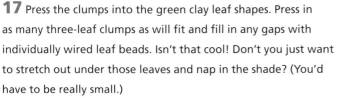

18 Roll out a little ball of clay, squeeze a little drop of liquid clay up in the sky, and press on the ball. Now press in the little metal button sun. There you go, pretty as a postcard!

19 Bake it for about 20 minutes to set everything, then gently turn it over and add a hanging loop (page 148). No need to add a patina to this piece, it's already perfect.

20 Finally, bake it again for the usual time. You may want to add a clear coating carefully to just the sunset, as the surface paint is easily nicked.

And now I have a sudden craving for pineapple and ukulele music!

Primordial Dance

Ammonite Fossil Pin

Size: 4" tall × 2½" wide
(10.2 × 6.4 cm)

For this project you will need:

- all the usual sculpting tools
- cutting blade
- 23-karat gold leaf (or gold metallic foil)
- liquid clay
- rhinestone crystals with heat backing (these are Swarovski HeatFix, 4mm in olivine and topaz)
- two half-cut fossilized ammonite shells (check the Resources, page 154)
- glue (two part epoxy, or other glue that can adhere to plastic and stone)
- pin back: 1¼" or 1½" (3.2 or 3.8 cm)

Eons ago when the ocean was young, ammonites ruled the deep. Luckily for us, they left their beautiful shells behind as fossils—wasn't that nice of them? This pin captures the poetic souls of those ancient creatures—dancing in the primordial sea. They were great dancers, you know.

Clay Recipe

1. Ocean color = ultramarine blue + green pearl (five or six parts blue to one part green) (amount: 1 oz.)

2. Background = gold (amount: 1 oz.)

3. Tentacle color = black + ultramarine blue (about three parts black to one part blue) (amount: 1 oz.)

1 When you mix up the ocean color, don't overmix (lookit! cool green streaks!). Now roll it through the pasta machine at the thickest setting to make a sheet.

With a cutting blade, cut out a fun shape, like this freeform rectangle.

2 Now roll out the gold clay into a thick sheet and lay the blue cutout right on top. Lay a piece of paper on top so you can rub it to connect the two without leaving a bunch of indentations from your heavy li'l hands. Now cut the gold clay out too, leaving a border around the blue. It doesn't need to be exact, it just needs to look cool.

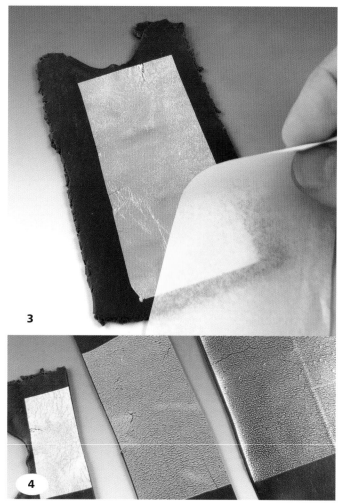

3

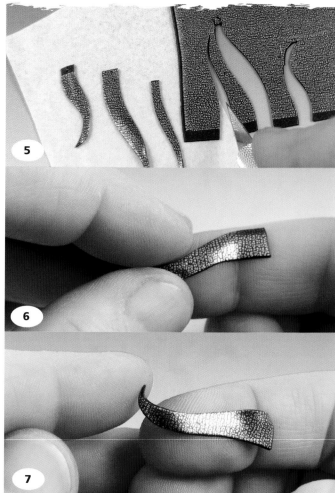

5

6

7

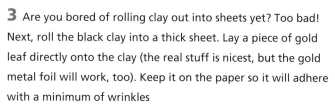

4

3 Are you bored of rolling clay out into sheets yet? Too bad! Next, roll the black clay into a thick sheet. Lay a piece of gold leaf directly onto the clay (the real stuff is nicest, but the gold metal foil will work, too). Keep it on the paper so it will adhere with a minimum of wrinkles

4 We'll make the ammonite tentacles from this metal-covered clay. It will look more interesting if we give the metal some crackle, so run the clay through the pasta machine at one notch smaller than the sheet is (you can cover the metal with the thin paper that the foil/leaf comes on to protect it during rolling). To increase the spacing of the crackle, roll the clay at thinner settings. I like to cut the initial sheet into thirds, keep one uncrackled, then make the other two different degrees of crackle—it adds some variety.

5 Now pick one of the sheets and cut out some tentacles! What, you've never cut out tentacles before? Oh, you've missed out on the fun! Use a sharp blade and cut a squiggly line. Now cut the other side to match—wider at one end and tapering to a point at the other—like little melting triangles. Mix and match the different crackle sheets for these.

6 Once you've made several, it's time to assemble them into an ammonite gently swaying in the currents. The first few of these tentacles can just be laid onto the clay flat, but the next few should be more rounded. To do that, just lay one of the tentacle slices on the length of your finger and press the outer edges down, giving it a curved look.

7 Hey, and why not curl some of the tips also!

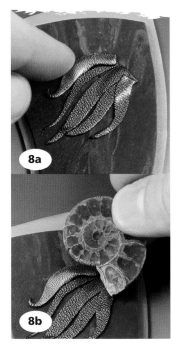

8a

8b

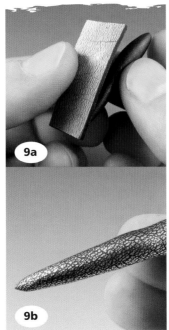

9a

9b

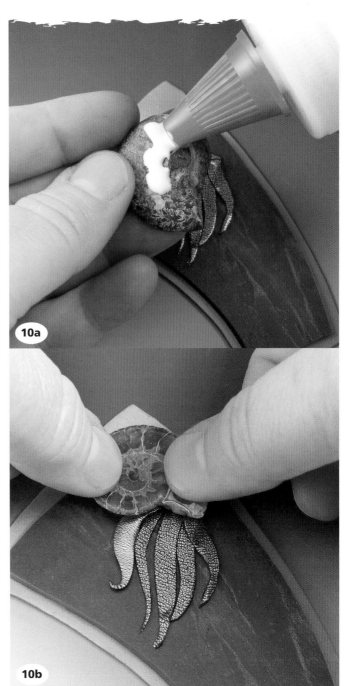

10a

10b

8 Now lay them down (flat ones first and curled ones on top). Just press them directly onto the blue clay. It helps to hold the ammonite shell up to the arrangement from time to time to make sure the tentacles aren't going beyond the width of the shell.

Once you have the tentacles wide enough, you'll have to build them up in height with a fat one or two so it looks as if those wavy arms are coming out of the shell.

9 From the black clay, roll out a snake that is about the same size as the rest of the tentacles. Lay a piece of the metal-covered clay on top of it, and then just roll them in your palms to smoosh them together into a thicker snake. Don't worry if there is lots of crackle in the gold; it'll look cool. Set these fatter tentacles aside for now.

10 Next, add the shell by pressing it down in place, then peel it up, add some glue, and replace it. You can use any glue that will adhere to plastic and stone. If you're not sure if the glue you plan on using will stay strong during the baking (some lose their grip in high heat), then just press the shell in and remove it after baking to add the glue then.

11a

11b

12

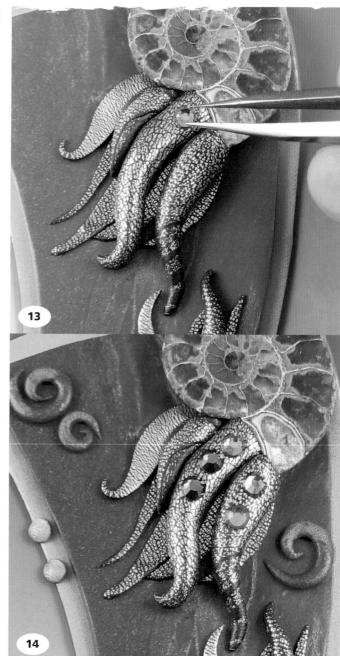

13

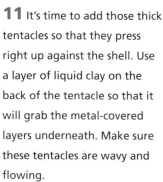

14

11 It's time to add those thick tentacles so that they press right up against the shell. Use a layer of liquid clay on the back of the tentacle so that it will grab the metal-covered layers underneath. Make sure these tentacles are wavy and flowing.

12 An ammonite shouldn't dance alone—so make another one down in the bottom corner. Same steps!

13 Even fossils need to look pretty, so this project is a good one to try out some crystal rhinestones. A few bits of bling on each ammonite will be just right, I think. Use flat-back rhinestones with a heat-activated glue backing. Just pick one up with some needle-nose tweezers and place it on the clay. Then use a small tool to press it firmly into the clay. The oven will do the rest!

14 All that's left are a few accents to make the picture complete. I suggest a few swirls and dots of clay to play up the oceany feel. Curls are thin snakes of clay, gently rolled up, and dots are dots!

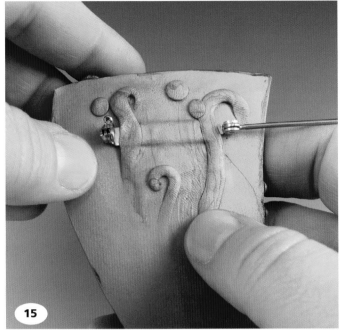

15 Since this will be a pin, it still needs some hardware on the back. First, give it a short bake to set all the details. Then, once it's cool, add the pin backing (page 148).

Now bake completely, cool, and add a touch of patina (I thought it only needed it on the gold clay), and a clear coating if desired.

Pin this onto your dancing blouse and sway to that primordial music!

Thor's Dragon-Serpent
Picture Frame

Size: 9" × 11" (22.9 × 27.9 cm)

When Thor was a boy, he had a beloved pet dragon-serpent, with spines forged from lightning bolts, and a body adorned with costly metals by the master smiths of the Craggen fjords. Throughout Thor's youth, he was never without his companion.

One day, the great golden eagle of Wodin swooped from the clouds, struck the dragon-serpent, and carried him off, amid great struggle and screeching, 'til the ground shook with their fury.

Thor and Wodin got together for a cup of coffee and agreed that their pets were certainly out of control, and they decided to raise bunnies instead from then on.

For this project you will need:

- all the usual sculpting tools
- craft knife
- wire cutters and pliers
- 28-gauge wire
- large, round, deep silver-colored bead for eye (this is a gray pearl)
- forks (antique, silver-plated is nicest, but anything that looks like it would work as dragon spine spikes will do just fine)
- accent beads in silvers and grays (these are pyrite crystals and gray button pearls)
- mica powder: silver (I used PearlEx 663 Silver)
- aluminum foil
- picture frame (this is a 5" x 7" [12.7 x 17.8 cm] wooden one)
- glue (any glue that will adhere to both wood and plastic)
- rock crystals (optional) (this is a cluster of apophyllite crystals)
- hacksaw
- drill, screwdriver, one wood screw (if possible)

Clay Recipe

1. Body = silver + pearl + burnt umber (two parts silver to one part each of the others) (amount: 6 to 8 oz.)
2. Accent = body color + black (amount: 1 to 2 oz.)
3. Accent = body color + gold (amount: 1 to 2 oz.)
4. Accent = body color + white (amount: 1 to 2 oz.)
5. Teeth = white clay (not pictured) (amount: 1 to 2 oz.)

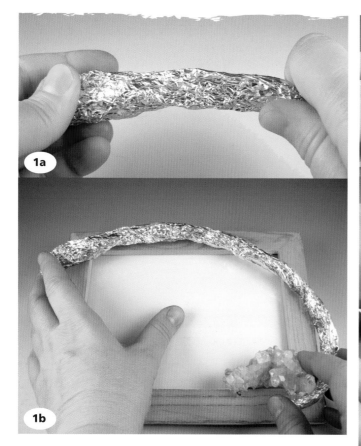

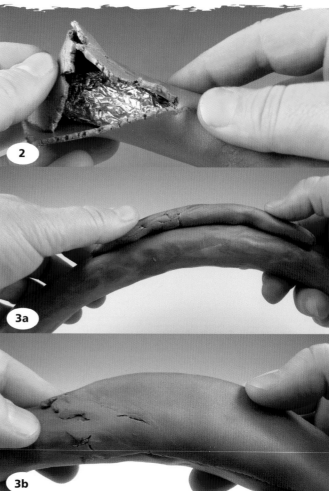

1 The size of your beastie will be determined by your picture frame, since he will stretch around the outer edge of the frame. Create an aluminum foil core that will be the innards of the dragon-serpent by ripping off a long sheet of foil and scrunching it into a snaky shape. Hold the foil up to the frame to decide the length and the pose. If you choose to incorporate a crystal, add that to the arrangement to get an idea of where it will go, and how the dragon-serpent will curve to accommodate it. This crystal is a piece of the mountains of the Craggen fjords. Or not.

2 Mix up enough of the body color clay to cover the whole foil core, with some left to make details with later. Run the mix through your pasta machine at the widest or almost-widest setting. Wrap the clay around the foil.

3 We're going to need some extra clay along the spine ridge to accommodate the fork spikes, so roll out a long log of clay, press it in place along his back, and then cover with another smaller sheet of clay. Smooth all of the clays together.

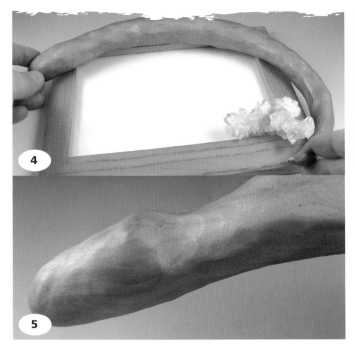

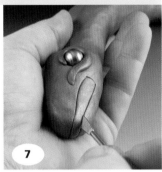

4 Smooth the whole shape from the head end to the tip of the tail. Place it on the frame again and adjust the curve as needed until you like the look. Set the frame aside; you won't need it anymore until the end.

5 To narrow the neck and enlarge the head, pull on the clay where you want the neck to be, making that clay bulge up onto the forehead area. Smooth it all once you've shaped it to your liking. If you need to, add additional clay to the forehead area and smooth into shape.

6 This dragon-serpent project was actually inspired by the Viking carving depicted below. That dragon graced a longboat and was probably the first thing many poor unfortunate folks saw as the invading warriors leaped from their vessels. I liked the large, staring eye and the toothy grimace. That's why this eye is large and metallic instead of more small, focused, and personal. Use a large bead, wire it up, and press it in. Make sure any visible wires are turned so that they will be covered by additional clay details. Use some of the accent clay colors and make those details next.

7 The mouth is serious, too. Trace an open mouth shape into the clay with a pointy tool.

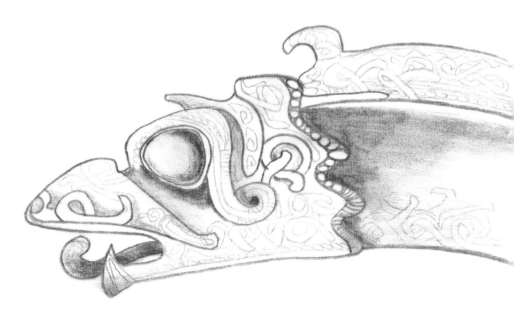

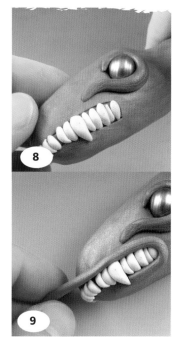

8

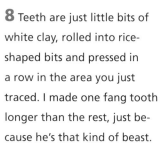

9

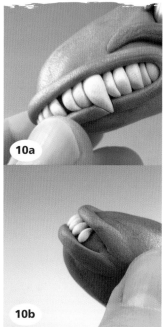

10a

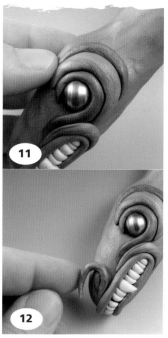

10b

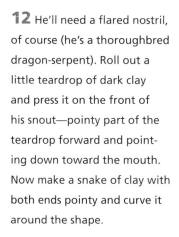

11

12

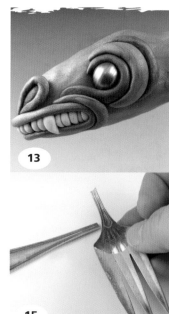

13

15

8 Teeth are just little bits of white clay, rolled into rice-shaped bits and pressed in a row in the area you just traced. I made one fang tooth longer than the rest, just because he's that kind of beast.

9 Clean up the mouth and hide the tops and bottoms of the teeth with a long log of clay for the lip. Start on the bottom of the mouth, right up to the fang (cut the log first so that it can press close to the tooth). Wrap the log around the corner of the mouth and along the top all the way to the back, out of sight, and pinch off the excess.

10 Slice the log again and press it against the front of that bottom fang and continue the lip around to the back. Pinch off the excess again and blend the two lip ends into the backside.

11 Add more details around the eyes and mouth, and just wherever you think it will look good.

12 He'll need a flared nostril, of course (he's a thoroughbred dragon-serpent). Roll out a little teardrop of dark clay and press it on the front of his snout—pointy part of the teardrop forward and pointing down toward the mouth. Now make a snake of clay with both ends pointy and curve it around the shape.

13 How's that face looking?

14 OK, now the back is going to be fun—a row of forks to create a bristling silvery sail of spines. Old forks, especially silver-plated ones, are the most fun—they add an ancient artifact look to the sculpture. I found a handful at an antique shop that looked nice and dragony.

15 Use a hacksaw to saw off the head of the forks with a bit of the neck left on.

19 OK, go nuts on the details now! Add clay accents of all the colors. Wire in and add the bead accents. Imagine what a metal-fork monster dragon-serpent should look like and go for it!

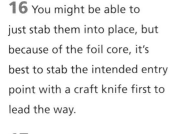

16 You might be able to just stab them into place, but because of the foil core, it's best to stab the intended entry point with a craft knife first to lead the way.

17 Jam in the cutlery—use the forks, Luke! (Sorry, bad *Star Wars* pun, I don't know what I was thinking.)

18 To add interesting detail, as well as to stabilize the forks, roll out some snakes of clay and press them around the forks and onto the body. Do that for all the forks.

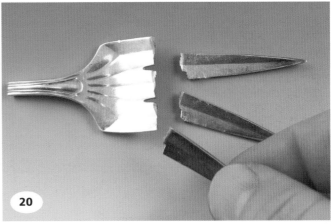

20 I saved one of the forks so I could use the tines individually as forehead spikes. Use the hacksaw to cut off each of the tines (or better yet, get your kids to do it for you, since it's a little harder than just hacking the fork head off).

21

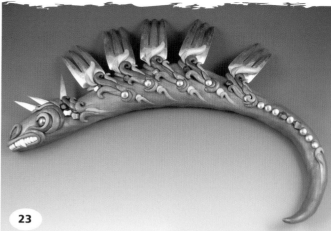

23

21 Press the tines into the forehead. Add clay to hold them steady, just as we did for the back forks.

22 Keep adding details of clay, and beads to body and tail and head!

22a

22b

22c

23 Looking good so far? Yeah, you know it!

24 Don't forget to make the tail fun. These are just some rice-shaped pieces clumped together, with a curled-up tip here and there.

25 Finally, add some mica powder in silver to tie the metal of the spines and beads all together.

26 Hmmm, he's is missing something. Ahhh, texture to the body! Just pokes with the edge of a dowel tool will do the trick, I think.

27 Go bake him for the full 45 minutes to an hour. You may need to use some paper or tissue to prop up the tail and forks to keep them stable.

24

25

26

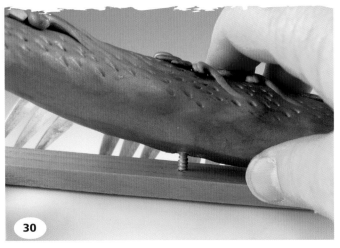

30 Now add your glue generously to the hole and press the dragon-serpent onto the screw. Add glue to secure the crystal (if you're using it in this assemblage), and glue where the tail touches the frame (if it does). Carefully weigh the clay piece down while the glue sets.

31 Pop in a picture of your favorite Viking, looking appropriately worried, to make this project something the Valkyries would be proud to hang up in Valhalla.

28 Add a patina if you wish. I think a deep blue looks particularly good on this guy.

29 Once he's cool, attach him to his picture frame. Since I am naturally distrustful of glue, I recommend a little extra something to make sure the connection is secure. So, lay the dragon-serpent on the frame and see where he will have contact with the wood. Mark the spot, and then screw a wood screw into the spot. With a drill, make a hole wide enough and deep enough to fit on top of the screw. Polymer clay is easy to drill into so don't be scared! (Just don't drill all the way through your beastie!)

Humans Being

Faces and People Parts

They say that we recognize even the most simplistic representation of the human face more quickly than any other image. (No, I don't know who "they" are, either, but they know these things.) No wonder the smiley face is an international icon. Humans have stylized themselves and their fellow humans throughout all cultures, from the first pigmented handprint pressed upon a rock wall.

In this section, we'll let mythology, archaeology, and nostalgia inspire us to create some fun people projects!

Aztec Head Focal Bead, *page 126*

Petroglyph Pebbles, *page 122*

**Embellished Transfer
Mini Flower Vase,** *page 132*

Face Heart Pendant, *page 138*

Rock On!
Petroglyph Pebbles

Size: 1" to 2" (2.5 to 5.1 cm)

For this project you will need:

- needle tool
- embossing powder in any dark color
- acrylic paint: dark brown (burnt umber or similar) + paintbrush and sponge

For some reason, mankind has always had this tendency to doodle on things—cave walls, big ol' rocks, colosseum walls, school desks. Petroglyphs refer to those doodles carved onto rocks, done long ago. Many, of course, are not just doodles, but had sacred or other significance to the humans who scratched them onto the rocks in the first place. The petroglyph pebbles in this project are not significant at all, unless of course you hide them somewhere to be discovered by archaeologists in the future who will attribute grave significance to them. It could happen.

OK, whether these will be in a museum eons from now or not, they're fun and easy to make and, for some reason, it's hard to stop once you get started! So be prepared for a tabletop covered with petroglyph pebbles.

Clay Recipe

1. Cernit nature color savanna (that's the beige one) = burnt umber, two parts savanna to one of burnt umber (amount: 1 oz.)

Begin by mixing your clay colors, of course. Your polymer pebbles will look most convincing if they have streaks and variations. (Think "river rock"—usually banded, speckled, or splotchy looking!). Use the Lookit blend method (page 18) to accomplish this (plus a little secret I'll tell ya about in a minute). The Cernit brand "nature colors" clay has some speckles blended into the mix already, so it's a nice choice if you have some, but don't worry if you don't. The colors you choose for your pebbles, and the amount of each you use, is up to your taste in rocks! I find it's nice to blend more than one version of the color, so the rocks will have more variety and look nicer if you group them together.

Use any of the following colors that you like, in any proportion: any of the Cernit clay nature color series works wonderfully. The other Premo colors that you can mix with Cernit, or use by themselves, are: white, pearl, silver, black, gold, burnt umber, copper, raw sienna, ochre, and beige.

Human Inspiration

Any of these images will work well for your pebbles. Or doodle your own! As you can tell, any stylized human figure will work well.

1 Let's make a pebble! Just pinch off a little wad of the color and roll it into a ball. Now flatten that ball in your palms as you continue to roll—it'll make a nice pebble shape.

Looks pebble-ish? Sorta? Well, OK, here's the secret I was hinting at earlier that will make it really rocky. You have to brush on and rub in some gritty stuff. There are several things you can use—glitter, embossing powders, even home seasonings like black pepper. I like embossing powder the best, myself. I have a little "rock" mix that I've made up of several colors including a "granite" one that adds whitish flecks to the surface of the pebble. When it bakes, it look like lichen, so that adds nice realism. Plus, embossing powders really stick to the clay, no flaking off after it's baked.

2 OK, once you pick your grit, use a brush or your fingertip to spread some over the surface of the pebble. Now roll the pebble in your palms again to firmly embed the grit into the clay, not just on the surface.

3

5

3 Wasn't that fun? OK, now to add the petroglyph image. You'll use a needle tool to scratch it into the surface. Usually I suggest using the edge of the tool, held almost horizontally, but for this, use the tip and scratch away! It will add to the ancient look.

You can just freehand the image straight onto the clay, or you can use a dowel tool to sketch it first onto the surface, rubbing out any wayward lines with your finger.

Scratch the design in fairly deeply, but don't worry if you can't see it really well right now—we'll fix that shortly.

Don't you wanna make a whole pile of them? OK by me!

4 OK, bake the pebbles in the usual way.

Let them cool completely.

5 To make the images more visible, you'll definitely want to add a patina of acrylic paint to fill in the scratches. For any medium- to lighter-colored pebbles, you should use a dark brown paint, like burnt umber. For really dark pebbles, you may want to fill in with a lighter paint, such as raw sienna or burnt sienna.

This is the same as any other patina you've done already—paint into all the cracks and crevices, and then wipe it off the surface with several barely damp sponges.

All done!

I think the pebbles look nice arranged in a group with a few real rocks thrown in. You don't have to tell anyone that they're not real, you know.

TIP: You can conserve the amount of clay you use, and keep the baking time down, by first making a core of aluminum foil. Wad up a bit of foil into a dense ball roughly the same shape as the pebble you wish to create. Now roll the clay mix through the pasta machine at the widest setting and rip it into a piece that will be large enough to wrap around the foil. Wrap it, squeeze to firmly attach, and roll the same way as you would if it were all clay.

Finishing Touches

- Patina—you've already done that!
- No clear coat is necessary—it would just take away from the rough rock look.

Quetzalcoatl Calls

Aztec Head Focal Bead

Size: head 1" (2.5 cm), total 3" (7.6 cm)

For this project you will need:

- all the usual sculpting tools
- craft knife
- small peacock feathers (or any small green/blue feathers)
- two beads for eyes: black onyx (or any similar dark, round 4mm beads)
- liquid clay
- gold leaf (23-karat gold, or gold-colored metallic leaf)—about one square inch
- embellishment beads: pearl, turquoise, 3mm Miyuki square glass beads (or any similar glass beads in greenish metallic finish)
- stone or glass donut-shaped disks: turquoise is preferable, but any green-colored ones will work fine
- small or extra-small beading cable (also called beading wire)
- 28-gauge wire
- 26-gauge or finer wire (preferably gold-colored or copper)

Feeling ancient, yet vibrant? If so, it's time to get in touch with your inner Aztec warrior (or priestess, or chieftain, depending on your mood). I've always been fascinated with the artistic richness of the ancient South American cultures. This focal bead is inspired by the artistry of those peoples. Quetzalcoatl was a god of that culture, often portrayed as a feathered snake. You have to admit, as gods go, that's a pretty cool persona!

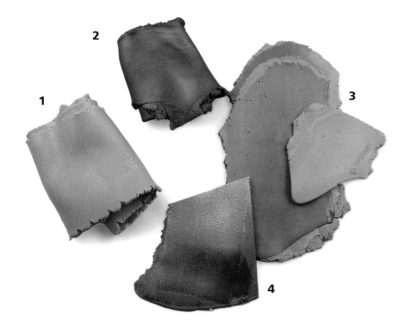

Clay Recipe

1. Flesh = ecru + copper (about three parts ecru to one part copper, you can add a little gold if you want it darker) (amount: 1 oz.)

2. Headdress = green pearl + gold (two parts green to one part gold) (amount: 1 oz.)

3. Turquoise = Cernit brand clay— "nature's colors" (basalt) + turquoise + ecru + white + green pearl + gold (mostly white and ecru, with just bits of the other colors—play around with it and see what you come up with!) (amount: 0.5 oz.)

4. Gold leaf on gold clay (amount: 0.5 oz.)

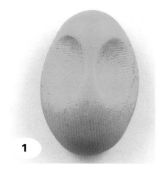

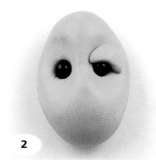

1 Begin by mixing up a flesh color. Mix the clays together thoroughly, no streaks. Roll out a ball of the color and shape it into a bit of an oval— this can be any size you'd like—about the size of a large grape will work well. Press your thumbs into the oval to create two indentations (the eye sockets).

2 Wire up the round eye beads and place each one in the center of the eye socket area. Embed the bead halfway into the clay, so that the wires are hidden in the clay. If you think the wires might show, turn the bead so that the problem wire is on the top, where the eyelid will cover it. Eyelids are just a little rice-shaped bit of clay, curved and laid above the eye bead.

(For more details on eyelids and their important role in conveying expressions, take a look at page 128!) I suggest the eyelids be positioned in a "contemplative, wisdom" setting (that's pretty much the same as the "I have no opinion" example).

3 Are you ready to pick your nose? (Oh dear, that can't be right.) The classic Aztec nose is unique. Ancient Aztec sculptures depict it often—aristocratic, distinctive. We'll go for a stylized version here, by making it longer than what you're probably used to. It will stretch up into the forehead area.

Make a rice-shaped bit of clay—twice as large as the eyelid—and flatten it slightly with your fingers. Press one end flat—this is the underside of the nose. Pull the tip down a little, keeping the ridge of the nose sharp.

Express Yourself!

When you're creating stylized human faces, the key to expression is all in the eyelids! Just the slightest shift in direction and angle changes the look completely! Where you place them and whether you add additional eye features (such as bottom lids or eyebrows) makes a big difference, as you'll see. The mouth plays a part, too, as you would expect—but the eyelids say it all! I purposely left off eyebrows, so you could see just how much expression you can convey with the lids alone. If you want to add the brows, they will echo the direction and shape of the eyelid, adding an extra emphasis to the emotion.

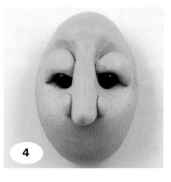

4

4 Now press it gently in place (keep the ridge of the nose sharp—don't let it mush). It should start at the forehead and run between the eyes. Now roll out two little balls of clay, place them on either side of the bottom of the nose, and press in place for nostrils.

All the details so far are just pressed on—nothing blended in—but feel free to gently blend in the lines if you prefer!

"I have no opinion. And you can quote me on that."

"Yikes! What are you going to do with that mallet?!"

"But you promised you'd buy me a pony …" <sniffffffffle>

"I'm so mad at you, but I can't remember why. Which just makes me even angrier! Grrrrr!"

"I'm so tired, I can't even keep my eyes opennn … zzzzzzzzz"

"Oh, my! Don't sneak up on me like that."

"Oh, mmmmm. Delicious chocolatey goodness … yum, yum, yum."

"Oooh, I'm so fiendishly clever—and you'll never guess what I put in your shoe."

5a

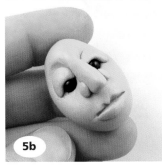

5b

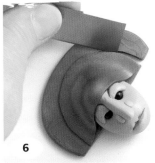

6

8

5 The mouth will be a bit more realistic—it will add to the whole aura of wisdom that this fellow embodies. Begin by using a pointed tool to impress a straight line in the mouth area. Now use the tool to press up and create a little notch on one side of the mouth—rounder in the middle, tapering to the line. Repeat the mirror image of this on the other side of the mouth. This is the upper lip. Notice again, this is stylized—we are not going for accuracy, just the proper feel of the lips. The bottom lip is added on. Make a rice-shaped piece as long as the mouth line and press it on, right along the opening. Blend it in at the sides and also along the top (a sharp-edged sculpting tool will help here—just run it gently back and forth in the mouth to smooth the clay of the mouth and the clay of the lip together).

6 OK, now for the fun part—costuming the dude! All feathers and necklaces and bling! Start by running some of the green clay mix through the pasta machine at several settings thinner than the wide setting. Now use a craft knife to cut out a half-circle shape. Place this right over his forehead, like a hat (which it is, kinda).

Cut a straight edge in the green clay. Now pick him up and place him on the green clay so that the straight edge lines up with the edge of the half-circle on his head. Press it down all around the outer edges, gently, but no smooshing. Trim away the excess from the bottom sheet to follow the curve of the top circle—he'll have a mushroom head at this stage.

7 Next, cut out a triangular shape, pick him up again, and press him down on the shape—this gives the hint of shoulders, and provides a place for all the necklaces to drape over.

8 Add ear disks (all the rage among the ancient Aztecs and Mayans, with good reason—they're pretty cool-looking!). Use the turquoise blend to roll out little balls of clay, flatten into pancakes, and press on in the ear area. The real ones were pretty huge and took over the whole side of the head—which works for us, because now we don't have to bother making ears!

Now the rest is really all up to your own fashion sense—I'll walk you through what I did, but feel free to follow your own ideas of what details should go where.

I thought a long strand of square beads (with smaller seed beads in between) looked groovy as a band across the top of the headdress. Make a strand of beads (page 147), and press them into place. Use clay if needed to secure the ends of the wire. Add a little wire "staple" to hold it down in the middle, since the strand is so long.

9

10a

10b

11

At this point, you can add a means of hanging the finished piece. Either use a needle tool to pierce a hole horizontally through the head (and insert a thicker wire to keep that hole open during the rest of the sculpting process), or add pendant loops of clay to either side of the head. These can look like a part of the finery, so it's a logical choice. Add them above the halfway point so the head won't tip forward. If it's going to be a wall piece, you can add a hanging loop to the back now, or after a short bake to set the piece (check those techniques in the back of the book for more info).

Feathers are next! In ancient South American cultures, as far as it is known, the amazingly long tail feathers of the quetzal were reserved for the nobility and royalty only, and their headdresses were pretty darn snazzy because of those feathers! We can't use those, of course, but these peacock feathers will substitute quite nicely. I think Montezuma's royal hairdresser would have approved.

9 Prepare the feathers and lay them directly on top of the clay. I think a fan of the feathers works well. Squirt a little liquid clay around the base of each feather.

10 Now just start adding details from all your clays. Cover the ends of the feathers with balls of clay. Use the turquoise-colored clay to add details wherever you like. Lay a piece of gold leaf on a sheet of gold clay and use a blade to cut out mosaic squares to add to the richness of the design. Wire up pearls and insert them as needed. One thing I recommend is to wire up a disc or two of turquoise and add it to the design—I especially liked one in the headdress and one on the neck. Just make him richly layered in colors, textures, and shapes!

11 Finally, he needs necklaces, lots and lots of necklaces! You can use regular 28-gauge wire, but if this will be a focal bead on a necklace, it's better if his necklaces are strung on something sturdier and less likely to break. Start by adding a crimp to one end of the cable (a refresher on this technique is on page 149).

12

13

12 Now string on the beads and then crimp off the other end when you've strung on enough, and trim off the excess. This first necklace should drape below the chest turquoise disk, framing it. Press each crimp into the clay with needle-nose tweezers. Add more clay as needed to give the crimps plenty to bury into.

13 Add as many necklaces as you'd like—the more, the better.

Bake as usual.

▲ This is a likeness of an actual sculpture of the Aztec/Mayan era. Note the mouth and nose that inspired this project.

◄ I stayed up all night to get my headdress just right—I sure hope the ladies notice me.

Finishing Touches

- Patina as needed: raw sienna on the face, burnt sienna and burnt umber in the headdress. Avoid the feathers.
- Clear coat if desired.

How Handy

Embellished Transfer Mini Flower Vase

Size 3½" tall × 2" wide (8.9 × 5.1 cm)

For this project you will need:

- all the usual sculpting tools
- cutting blade
- scissors
- liquid clay
- laser transfer of vintage image
- assorted accent beads: glass and/or carved stone flowers, crystals, pearls, seed beads
- headpins, regular and decorative
- small glass medicine bottle, preferably antique (browse through an antique, collectibles, or thrift shop and I bet you'll find several!)

Adding a transferred image to polymer clay is a world of fun, and this project will only touch on what you can do with this technique. There are also several different ways to transfer an image onto clay, so if you are interested in doing more of this sort of thing, check the back of the book for some more suggestions. The really fun part of this project is embellishing the transfer, adding a dynamic, dimensional quality.

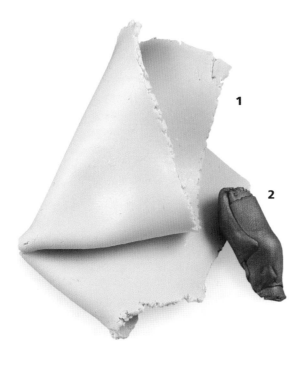

Clay Recipe

1. Transfer background color = equal amounts white + pearl (amount: 1.5 oz.)

2. Accent for sleeve = equal amounts red pearl + gold (amount: 0.25 oz.)

1 You'll need a transfer of an interesting vintage image. Here's the process I went through. First, I wandered around my local antiques store until I found this fun old calling card.

2

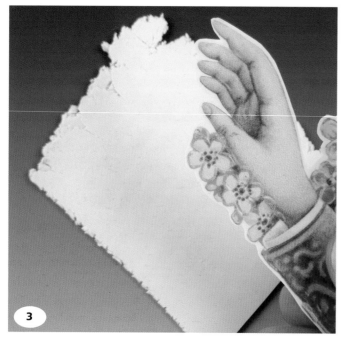

3

4

5

2 Then, I digitally altered the image to suit my needs. (If you're not a computer graphics person, you can do a similar job if you're handy with scissors and glue.) This is what I came up with. You can use it if you want to, I don't mind! (Just copy from this page, or for a free download, check the Resources section in the back of the book for details.)

3 OK now, what to do with the image? How to make a transfer? One of the easiest ways is to have a laser color copy made (most copy centers or office supply stores will offer this service). You have to have a laser copy so the colors won't run when the image gets wet.

Trim your transfer closely all around, leaving just a tiny border.

4 Now run the white clay through the pasta machine at the widest setting. Take the transfer and lay it onto the surface of the clay and rub on the paper backing to make sure it's stuck on.

5 Now go soak your hand! No, the transfer hand, silly. Use lukewarm water (not hot). Let it soak for about 10 minutes.

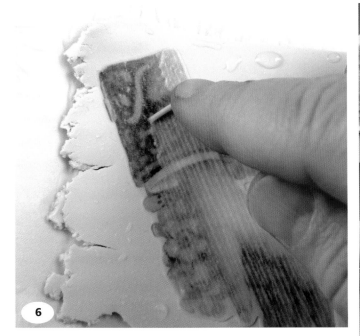

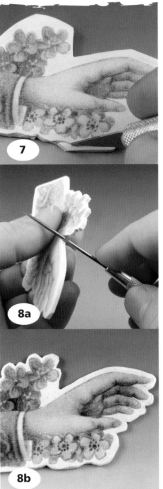

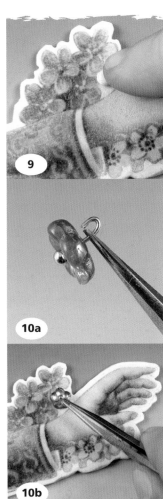

6 Pull the clay plus transfer out and set it on the paper towel. Use your fingertip to rub until the paper backing starts coming off (the water will have gotten it all soggy by now). You won't get it all off on the first rub, so dump out the cool water, refill with lukewarm water, and plonk the clay back in for another five or ten minutes. Next, back onto the paper towel and rub some more. Do this as many times as you need to until no more paper comes off and just the lovely transferred image is left. If you want a more "nostalgic" look, you can leave on a thin fuzz of paper (that's just a nice way to say it'll look old, which, after all, works well with this particular image).

7 Once you have the paper off to your liking, pat the clay dry with paper towels (oh, and you can ditch the bowl of water now, too). Now use a sharp cutting blade to trim all around the image, leaving a little border of clay showing around the edges.

8 Use your fingers to smooth the cut lines, and a tool to get in the hard-to-reach places, such as the deeper angles. There, isn't that nice?

9 Now the fun part! To add embellishment beads, we'll need a little extra clay for those wires to hide in. Roll a small ball of clay, add a drop of liquid clay to the transfer where you want the clay to go so it will grab, and press into place firmly.

10 Now prepare an embellishment (this one's a glass flower bead), using a headpin with the end bent up (remember, this trick is in the back of the book). Now press the bead into the little clay ball. Press firmly!

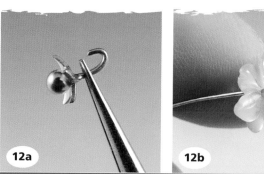

11 I thought a good place to start would be adding more flowers on top of the flower images in the design, so I used carved gemstone flowers, glass flower beads, and Swarovski crystals to create a cluster of blue and purple floral sparkles.

12 Ready to embellish the orangey flower section next? Prepare the flower beads in the usual way, as well as some decorative head pins. Hey! Let's use some of those flat heat-set crystals, too! Don't forget to add the little balls of clay wherever you need to embed the wires.

◀ You could mirror the image of the hands and make two holding the vase.

13 A row of deep burgundy-red pearls would go nicely with the jacket cuff, so why not add those right about now?!

14 Since the clay sheet is thin, even with the added balls of clay, you may find that the wire pokes through the back sometimes. If that happens, just patch it with little round "pancakes" of clay!

15 This original image has little brassy gold dots decorating the sleeve. Cut the tips off some gold headpins to trace those accents. Just press them right in. If there was enough room on the bitty little wire, I'd recommend bending in the little hook at the end, but we can't with these, so just press them in place and use your power of positive thinking to make sure they stay put. See, it's working! (You can also add a tiny drop of glue afterward if your powers start to wane. Hypo-Cement comes with a thin nozzle just right for this delicate work, but glue on a toothpick works too.)

16 As a final touch, I thought the end of the arm would look nice with some clay whoop-dee-doodles to set it off. First add a thin line of liquid clay for the new clay to grab onto. Now make some dots and curls and press them gently on top of the liquid clay. Ahhh, now that's just right. And it's complete. Wasn't that fun?

Bake the piece for a bit shorter than most since it's so thin—30 minutes is plenty. Add a clear coating on top of the clay if you want to, but it will change the look. I left mine uncoated to keep it looking antique.

Finally, glue it onto the little medicine bottle and add a sprig of something old-fashioned, like lilac or cherry blossoms. Doesn't that make you want to loosen your corset and put down the mending for a slice of warm huckleberry pie?

All Screwed Up

Face Heart Pendant

Size: 2½" (6.4 cm) tall

**For this project
you will need:**

- all the usual sculpting tools
- one glass eye
- one screw
- 16- or 18-gauge wire—2" (5 cm),
  for pendant loop

This heart pendant can be worn when you're having "one of those days" to let everyone know to steer clear. Or add a ribbon to the pendant loop and dangle it from the car mirror of your teenage daughter's car as a warning to any would-be boyfriends that she has a protective parent at home. Or tie it around a chocolate bar and give it to a friend who's going through a rough time—she'll have a chuckle and a chocolate, and things won't seem so bad anymore.

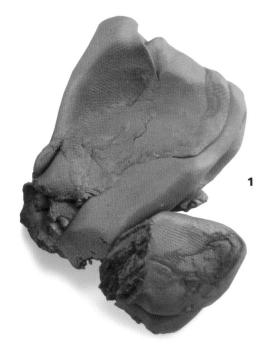

1

Clay Recipe

1. You can make this heart out of any color you want. If you like this color, it's equal parts copper and gold + a smidgen of orange (amount: 1 oz.)

hair

♡

bling

pink
big lips

grrr

black
heart

flowers

beads

groovy!

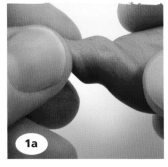

1a

1b

1 Make a heart shape. To make the twist on the tip, press the tip just a little between your finger and thumb to flatten it. Twist that to make a corkscrew—twist, slide your fingers down and twist more, and repeat until you run out of heart! Just a few twists should do it!

▲ Faces, faces, faces—so many possibilities. Pink heart to go with a smiley, girly face—add some "bling" crystals. How about two hearts in love—that's redundant, but it could work. Hair—spiky and off to the side. And on and on and on we go …

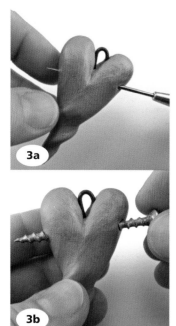

3a

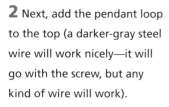

3b

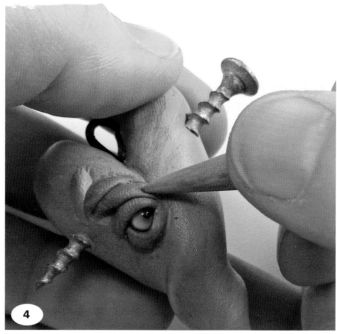

4

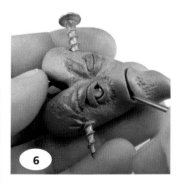

6

2 Next, add the pendant loop to the top (a darker-gray steel wire will work nicely—it will go with the screw, but any kind of wire will work).

3 Use a needle tool to make a guide hole for the screw. Make sure you avoid the pendant wire if you can, and insert the tool at a slight diagonal to make it more dramatic. Pull out the needle tool, place the tip of the screw in the hole, and twist—it will screw right into the clay!

4 This character has only one eye because the face is going to be all squinty, and if you remember your Popeye cartoons, just one eye makes the squinty face look just right! I used a special glass lampworked eye (see the Reference section in the back for more details), but a glass doll's eye will work, too. As you press in the eye, angle the pupil of the eye toward the screw, for even more drama! Remember to press the eye in deeply. Add the brows and lids by using little rice-shaped bits of clay. A lid above and below the eye is good for that puffy look. Add another lid (or brow, or whatever it is) above in the "angry" position—aimed down toward the nose (if he had one, which he doesn't. So then how does he smell? Just as bad as ever).

5 The other "eye" is all lids and creases. Just press them on. Two lids like the other eye, only placed one on top of the other—since this eye is closed, no eyeball will show. Add another angry eyelid or two to really make sure the attitude is noticeable. Press the lids firmly onto the clay heart to attach, and smooth all around the edges if you want to.

6 Now he'll need a mouth to really sell the look. Impress a line into the clay with the tip of a needle tool—slightly offset toward the open eye is best. Use the needle tool, or a dowel tool, to pull open that grimace in one corner a little bit more. There. Now, that's a screwed-up face!

7 Finally, use the rounded tip of a tool to press in little dimples of clay for an interesting texture, if you want to.

Bake as usual.

Finishing Touches

- Patina to bring out the lines of the face: use a darker brown such as burnt umber. You could even use a deep green paint to create a verdigris look.
- Clear coating if desired, on the clay only.

Want to make some more face hearts?
Here are some ideas to get your wheels turning!

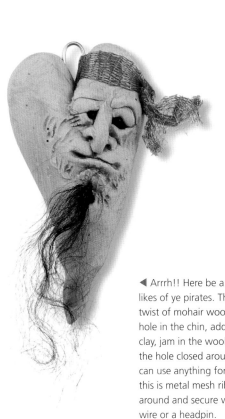

◀ Hyuck, hyuck! He's not really stupid, it's just that nobody takes him seriously on account of them gooooogly eyes. To make the mouth for this one, press an oval of clay onto the mouth area and open it up with a dowel tool. Jam in a lineup of several pearls or beads for his teeth!

◀ Arrrh!! Here be a heart for the likes of ye pirates. The beard is a twist of mohair wool—just poke a hole in the chin, add some liquid clay, jam in the wool, and squeeze the hole closed around the hair. You can use anything for the bandana; this is metal mesh ribbon—just wrap around and secure with a "staple" of wire or a headpin.

▶ Heavenly lips—for that angel in your life. The halo is one link of a brass necklace and jammed into the clay, which doubles as the hanging loop. For the lips, make the usual two rice-shaped bits placed together—but to make that silicone fullness on the top lip, press a little indentation into it first.

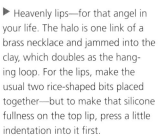

▶ There's always a smart aleck somewhere in the group, isn't there? Make the tongue out of a little teardrop of clay and use a needle tool to press a line down the center. The hair is just golden embroidery thread.

◀ Bling time! Use bicone crystals on head pins (you know how to do that) and jam 'em in all around for a real appealing glitzy look!

Gallery

More Ideas to Feed Your Imagination

◄ This Green Guardian figure really puts it all together by incorporating lots of mixed media! The face and wings are polymer clay, of course (and I used those fun glass eyes again, as we did in the screwy heart). The hair is raw wool, with sphagnum moss all mixed in, as you would expect from one of Mother Nature's gal pals. Metal leaves are combined with beads and ribbon for her foliage-themed accents. The wings incorporate ammonites, and the feathery details have been penciled on after the polymer was baked, with a clear coating to keep them from smudging.

What makes this sculpture easy is that the armature is just a glass jar with the wings and head secured to the jar with duct tape and wire. To hide all the tape and wire mess, the fabrics were soaked in Paverpol and draped on top of the jar and around the wings. Paverpol is a product especially designed to make fabric drape and stiffen beautifully, as you can see.

Want to make this Green Guardian? Ooops, no room in this book for the project, but don't worry, you can download the project online. Check out the Resources section for more details.

▶Use a tool to drag the surface of the added clay bits to create a painterly looking blend.

Little jade and malachite beads jazz up this small forest floor bead.

◀ The flower cluster is comprised of carved carnelian flowers and seed beads on headpins.

◀ Hemp twine is tucked into the clay mane and chin.

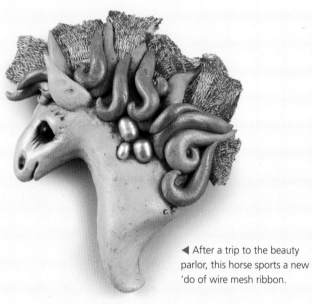

◀ After a trip to the beauty parlor, this horse sports a new 'do of wire mesh ribbon.

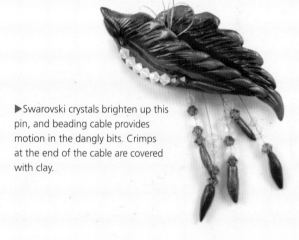

▶ Swarovski crystals brighten up this pin, and beading cable provides motion in the dangly bits. Crimps at the end of the cable are covered with clay.

▶ Use the circle bead wire method to make the flowerlike accents in this tree.

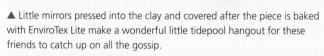

▲ Little mirrors pressed into the clay and covered after the piece is baked with EnviroTex Lite make a wonderful little tidepool hangout for these friends to catch up on all the gossip.

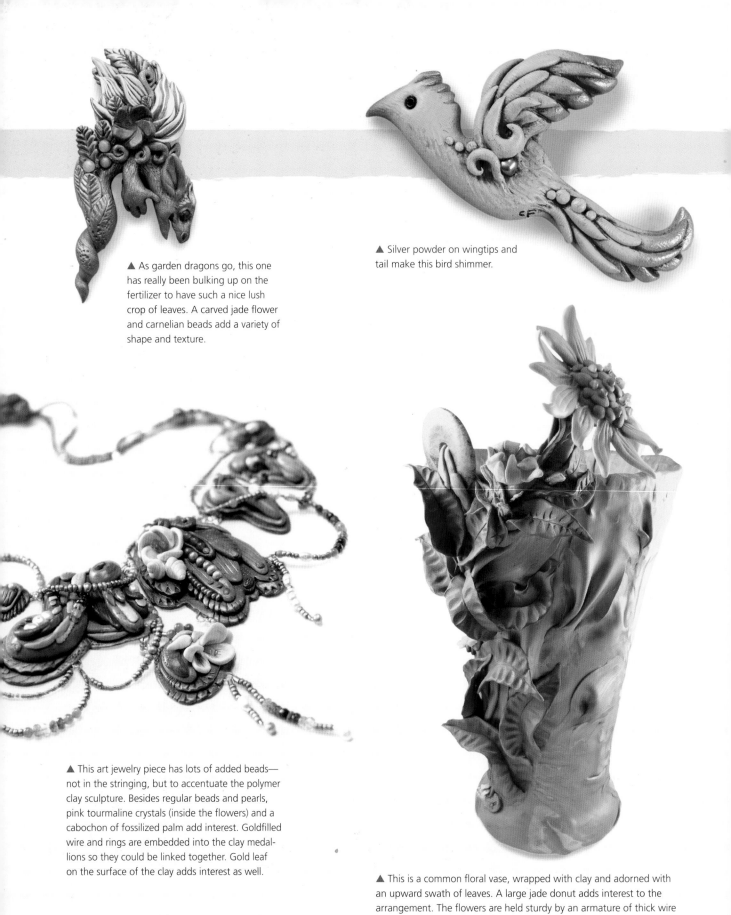

▲ As garden dragons go, this one has really been bulking up on the fertilizer to have such a nice lush crop of leaves. A carved jade flower and carnelian beads add a variety of shape and texture.

▲ Silver powder on wingtips and tail make this bird shimmer.

▲ This art jewelry piece has lots of added beads—not in the stringing, but to accentuate the polymer clay sculpture. Besides regular beads and pearls, pink tourmaline crystals (inside the flowers) and a cabochon of fossilized palm add interest. Goldfilled wire and rings are embedded into the clay medallions so they could be linked together. Gold leaf on the surface of the clay adds interest as well.

▲ This is a common floral vase, wrapped with clay and adorned with an upward swath of leaves. A large jade donut adds interest to the arrangement. The flowers are held sturdy by an armature of thick wire that extends from the flower head all the way down the side of the vase to the base. You can use duct tape or masking tape to hold the wire in place before adding the sheets of clay to cover the glass. Bake it right in.

▶There are a lot of mixed-media additions to this necklace. The metal leaves are electroplated copper—wonderful additions to the leaves of clay. Of course, lots of added beads. The set stone has a loop on the top (it was a pendant) so it wires into the clay firmly—the clay leaf above it hides the wires. The jewels on the dragonfly's body were cut from a bracelet and the details of clay hold it in place without detracting from the design. The dragonfly's wings are translucent clay and have been gently dry-brushed with white acrylic paint once the piece was baked.

◀ This proud peacock may not be winging it because just hanging around is impressive enough. Headpins hold up the clay for the crest. Swarovski crystal beads jazz up the tail, gold mica powder on the beak.

▲ A faceted carnelian set in a sterling silver bezel was snipped off a necklace to grace this dragon's shoulder. The pearls are held in with headpins.

▲ You can never have too many penguins. These fellas have semiprecious stone eyes.

Tips and Techniques

Stuff You Gotta Know

Here's the info that you need to sneak to the back of the book to find (this kind of cheating is perfectly acceptable, of course). For most things, this is just the way I do it after years of trial and error, or from minutes of asking others who know what they are doing how they do it.

Wiring Beads

To add beads to clay, a wire "tail" is needed to secure them. There are several ways to wire beads to achieve different looks. I have found that the best wire to use is 28-gauge.

WIRING UP A SINGLE BEAD

1. Thread a bead onto a snippet of wire (about 2" [5 cm] or so).

2. Pull the wires together, parallel, and grip the wires with pliers about ½" (1.3 cm) or less from the bead.

3. Twist the bead with your fingers until it is firm against the bead.

4. Snip away the wire to leave a short tail of about ¼" (6 mm). For an extra-secure hold, bend the tip of the wire back into a fishhook shape, embed the bead into the clay—wire side first, of course—and press the bead into the clay so that it is partially covered with no wire showing if possible.

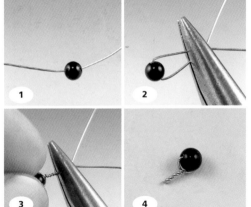

WIRING UP A DONUT-SHAPED BEAD

1. Wrap wire around and around the donut.

2. Pull the wires tight, grip them with pliers, and twist.

3. Trim off the excess tail and bend a little fishhook in the end.

4. Press the wire into the clay. You can leave the wire exposed or you can cover it with a ball or curl of clay. Support the back of the donut with a ball of clay for stability.

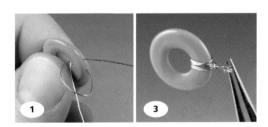

MAKING A CIRCLE OF BEADS

Use a disk or lentil-shaped bead for the best look, but round beads will also work. Avoid long beads, as the wire will show in an icky kind of way.

1. String on the beads—usually five to seven beads works well—and pull the wires together.

2. Grip the wires with pliers and twist, just as you did for wiring a single bead.

3. Snip off the excess wire and bend the wire perpendicular to the circle of beads; add a fishhook bend at the end.

4. Press the wire straight in. Hide any exposed wire with a clay detail.

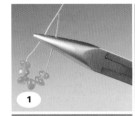

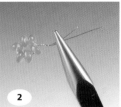

WIRING A STRAND OF BEADS

1. Snip off a 2"–3" (5–7.6 cm) length of wire and bend a fishhook in one end.

2. Thread on some beads—usually 1" or 1½" (2.5 or 3.8 cm) is the optimal; any longer and the strand is too wobbly.

3. Snip off any excess wire from the other end and bend in another fishhook.

4. With needle-nose tweezers, push one end of the beads into the clay.

5. Push the beads down onto the surface of the clay. Grab the other end with the tweezers, keeping the beads lined up tightly, and push the other end of the wire into the clay. Allow a slight arch in the lineup of beads.

6. Press the lineup down into the clay, flattening the arch and burying the beads at either end slightly.

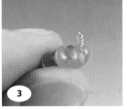

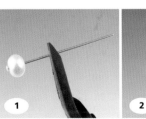

USING A HEADPIN TO SECURE BEADS

This is a great method of adding a different angle to the bead accents. Remember that you will see the head of the pin, so incorporate that into the design!

1. Thread the bead onto the headpin; snip the end off the pin, leaving only about ¼" (6 mm).

2. Bend a fishhook into the end; press the bead directly into the clay, hook first.

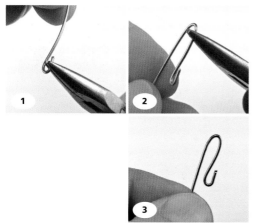

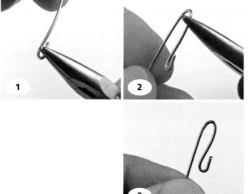

Hanging loops

MAKING WIRE PENDANT LOOPS

Add one to the clay to create a loop for stringing when the piece is done.

1. Cut off a piece of wire about 2" (5 cm) long; grip the tip of the wire in your pliers and bend the wire around the tip of the pliers into a hook (now it should look like a J).

2. Regrip the wire with the pliers about ½" (1.3 cm) above the hook; bend the wire over the pliers. Bend all the way over until both wires are parallel.

3. Snip off the remaining wire to leave the unbent end slightly longer than the bent end. You do not need to bend a J in both sides; just one will hold the wire loop in the clay securely. Press into the clay until only the loop is showing.

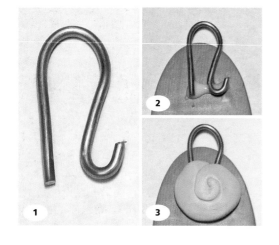

ADDING A WIRE HANGING LOOP TO THE BACK

It's always best to partially bake the piece first and then add this hanging hook to the back.

1. Bend the wire into a hook with at least one end folded back on itself (use the same process as above with the pendant loop).

2. Add liquid clay to the baked clay surface where the pendant will be attached. (For balance, two hangers are recommended—one in each corner.)

3. Cover the liquid clay with fresh clay and bake.

Adding a heat-back crystal rhinestone

Just press it in place on the unbaked clay and bake! The heat will activate the glue backing.

Adding a hinged straight-pin backing

First partially bake the piece before adding the pin backing.

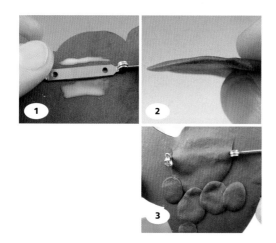

1. Spread out a thin layer of liquid clay where the pin will be added; open the pin and press the back onto the liquid clay.

2. With the same color clay if possible, roll out very thin bits of clay.

3. Press them on top of the pin backing, sandwiching it between the fresh and baked clay, press firmly all around; bake to secure the pin in place.

Removing the wire to open the stringing channel

Just yank it out. Kidding! If it's loose, of course that will work, but otherwise hold the wire with pliers (not with your fingers!) and twist the wire to break its grip (you'll probably hear a little "pop" sound). Gently pull the wire out with the pliers, a little at a time. Be patient!

Using beading wire and adding crimps

Beading wire (also called beading cable) comes in a variety of colors, styles, and sizes. Usually a medium-size wire will work with any clay-related projects. The more strands in the cable, the more flexible and less prone to kinking it will be.

For securing a closure on a necklace, use a crimp. You can also add a crimp to give clay a place to grab. Use a crimp bead or crimp tube and crimping pliers for the best success.

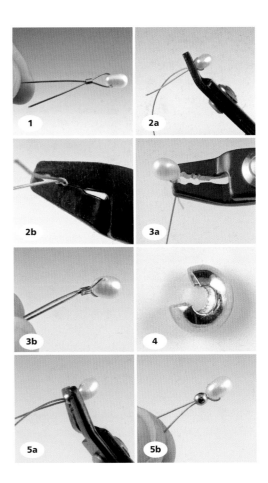

1. To dangle a bead at the end of beading wire, thread on the crimp bead and then the bead. Loop the short end of the wire back through the crimp bead.

2. Pull the crimp close to the bead with the crimping pliers. To create the crimp in the bead, use the back groove of the pliers and press firmly. This will make a bend in the crimp bead.

3. Now regrip the bent bead with the forward groove of the pliers and press very firmly to fold the bead on itself at the crimp. If done correctly, this will hold the wire very firmly—give it a good tug to make sure.

4. If the crimped bead will be visible in the design, it's always nice to hide it under a crimp cover.

5. Just place the cover over the crimp and use pliers to bend the cover closed. Isn't that clean looking?

Adding a patina and a clear, protective coating

Adding a patina merely means adding a coloring to the surface of a finished piece. This step is always optional, but it usually enriches the look of the clay (making it richer and less chalky looking), as well as bringing up all the details. It is essentially the same as antiquing. I love this step! It's boring and tedious, but the results are always worth it.

1. Start by mixing your paint. Use acrylic paints (any brand will do, I'm partial to Liquitex acrylics). Keep the mix thick, like the consistency of mayonnaise. You can use the paint straight from the tube or mix a custom color.

2. Use a paintbrush to cover a small section at a time with the paint. Acrylic dries quickly, so work small and fast! Use the brush to force the paint down into all the cracks and creases and texture areas. It's OK to brush over the beads (although you may want to avoid clear crystals, as paint trapped under them tends to dull the reflected sparkle). Avoid painting over any porous medium, like wool or feathers.

3. With a damp sponge (very wrung out so that it's barely damp) wipe off the surface paint. Throw that sponge in a bowl of water, get the next sponge and wipe again, toss that one in the water, take another sponge and get the last of the surface paints wiped off so that the paint remains only in the creases. The key to this is many sponges. You don't want to use just one or two and end up just smearing the paint all around, which just makes the surface muddy. Ick!

4. Continue until the whole piece is finished. Rinse out the sponges as you go along. You can also just patina spots here and there as needed. Varying the colors of paint used in each area of the piece is also useful—some areas may need a light color and others dark. My favorite color to patina with is brown as it really imparts an organic look to the clay, which works for me. You may have your own favorite color scheme or palette. I use raw sienna, burnt sienna, and burnt umber for almost all of my pieces.

5. Once the patina is finished, let it dry. If you'd like to add a clear coating, use a brush to cover the surface of the piece (except for the beads—don't add any clear coating over the beads, as it will actually dull the surface of most beads either immediately or over time). By the way, you do not need to add any patinas or any clear coatings—the clay is just groovy without them!

6. If you did add a clear coating, let the clear coat dry as well, then pop the piece back in the oven for 15–20 minutes at 225°–250°F (100°–120°C) to set all the surface treatments.

A word about clear coatings, varnishes, glazes and so on. A number of products work well with polymer clay—and a number are disasters! All of the major clay manufacturers have glazes that of course all work beautifully with polymer clay. A number of other varnishes do as well—such as some floor waxes and some outdoor varnishes. My favorite clear coating is a Rustoleum brand Varathane (satin diamond finish, water based). Product style #200261—it's available online and at some hardware stores. Check the Resources section for more sources).

Clear coatings have different amounts of shine, high gloss being the most glass like effect, and satin and matte being the dullest shine. Most of these projects are very organic and natural, so the lower the shine the better!

Glues

There are many glues available, and I don't claim to be an expert on what works best. Remember that polymer clay is a plastic and you should use a glue that will adhere to plastic, if adding anything to your clay with glue. I use two-part epoxys, superglues, and a few others when I need glue. If you can, try to embed the accent/embellishment into the clay piece in some other way than gluing it on afterward. Anything baked into the clay will probably be more durable than anything added to the surface after baking.

Cutting glass and mirrors

This allows you to customize the size and shape of the glass/mirror. Glass cutters are cheap, and available from any hardware store.

1. Lay the glass on a hard, flat surface. Press the wheel of the cutter firmly on the surface of the glass and move steadily in the line you wish to cut. Listen for the crackle that let's you know the glass is being properly scored. Use safety glasses for protection.

2. Carefully pick up the glass. With the ball end of the cutter, firmly tap the underside of the glass all along the scored line. The glass should fall apart at the line. If it's stubborn, you may pull the glass apart with pliers.

3. Take the sharp edge off the cut with several swipes of a carborundum stone, if possible.

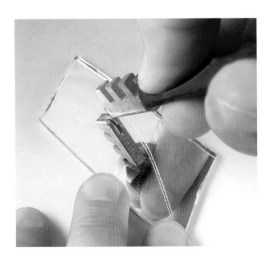

Wrapping a mirror in clay

This is a nice trick to create a surface around a mirror to make it ready for added decorations.

1. Start by putting clay through your pasta machine at a medium setting.

2. Lay your mirror on top and trim the clay all around your mirror, leaving a border of ½" (1.3 cm) or more.

3. Wrap the clay over the edges of the mirror. That's it!

Wrapping a glass jar in clay

This also readies the vessel for additional clay (and mixed media) embellishments.

1. If the jar has threads, first cover them with a strip of flattened clay.

2. Set your pasta machine at a medium setting and roll out several sheets. Pinch the top of a sheet together in a loose pleat, tuck it inside the jar, and press it onto the inside surface of the glass. Wrap it up and over and under the bottom.

3. Repeat with more sheets until the entire glass surface is covered. Leave the overlapping seams as they are, or blend them together with your thumb or with a tool. It's done, and ready for embellishing!

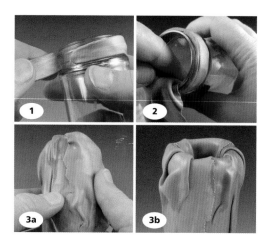

Clay brands

Well, here's a fitting place to wrap up—with the beginning! We started with clay and let's end with clay. There are several major brands of polymer clay. Each of those companies comes up with new types of clays, reformulations of existing clays, and tempting combo packs. Here are the major brands of clay and just a little about them to guide you to choosing the one that works best for you.

For sculpting purposes, any of the brands may be mixed together. So experiment, play, and create!

▲ Kato Polyclay is also a firm clay. Not as difficult to condition as classic Fimo, but still takes a bit of muscle. Again, very durable and great for holding details.

▲ Fimo is a firm clay that is more work to condition, but bakes up to be an extremely durable clay. Fimo Soft conditions easier and still retains that durable finished product. Especially good for holding small details in caning, modeling, and miniature work.

▲ Cernit is a softer clay with all-around uses. I especially love its "nature colors" line, which has flecks in the clay that make a nice addition to earthy blends.

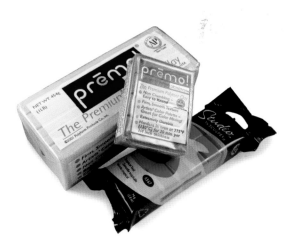

▲ Premo and Sculpey are the two major offerings from Polyforms. They have also just added a Studio line of clay. Premo is my very favorite clay because it is just perfect for sculpting! It conditions easily and is durable when baked.

Sculpey is a soft clay, the least durable clay when baked. It is an especially good clay to use when working with children who find the soft clay easy to work with.

Studio clay is a new clay and is very good to use when working with molds and stamps, as it releases quickly and cleanly and doesn't leave much residue sticking to the mold surfaces.

Resources

Supplies

Here is some information to lead you in the right direction! These are some sources for finding the things that you need for these projects (and whatever other ones you find yourself creating!).

CLAYS, AND CLAY TOOLS

There are a lot of places to get polymer clays—most craft stores carry the major brands, many bead stores do, too. Online sources are easy to order from as well. Things that go with clay, including tools and powders are usually available from the same places. Here are a few of my favorites:
www.ClayFactory.net (California), phone: (877) 728-5739
www.PolymerClayExpress.com (Maryland), phone: (800) 844-0138

By the way, Polymer Clay Express carries the small containers of Flecto Verathane, my favorite clear coating/varnish!
www.CreativeWholesale.com (Georgia), phone: (800) 347-0930

TOOLS, WIRE, JEWELRY FINDINGS, AND BEADS!

Again, craft stores and bead stores are a great place for most of your needs. These are a few of my favorite places to get these items:
www.FireMountainGems.com (Oregon), phone: (800) 423-2319
www.ThunderbirdSupply.com (New Mexico), phone: (800) 545-7968
www.RioGrande.com (New Mexico), phone: (800) 545-6566

SPECIALTY BEADS AND OTHER SPECIAL ITEMS

A few of many great places for special, nifty seed beads:
www.BeyondBeadery.com (Colorado), phone: (800) 840-5548
www.EastofOz.com (New York), phone: (718) 798-7961

One of my favorite sources for nice Venetian beads as well as that fun metal mesh ribbon, and great fabric ribbons, too:
www.SpecialtyBeads.com (California), phone: (530) 582-4464

Another source for the mesh ribbon, also called wire lace, is:
www.AlaCarteClasps.com (California), phone: (800)-977-2825

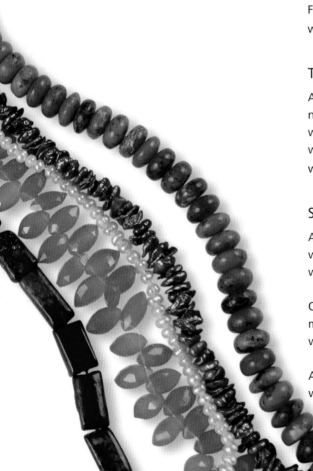

Great pearls can be found at many locations; try one of my favorites:
www.EastWestBest.net (California), phone: (415) 504-7338

Remember those fun enamel beads, disks, and rings from the Love
'em and Leaf 'em project? Those are from artist Sara Lukkonen.
Find them at:
www.CkoopBeads.com (Minnesota), phone: (218) 525-7333

The electroformed metal leaves used in the Green Guardian sculpture
can be found at:
www.RealmOfTheGoddess.com (California), phone: (323) 525-1085

MIXED MEDIA AND CRAFT SUPPLIES

Of course you can scour craft stores, hobby stores, scrap booking
shops, yard sales, thrift stores, antique shops, and online for all kinds
of things to use with polymer clay projects. Here are also two of the
larger online craft sellers that will have all your paints, pencils, glues,
and lots of mixed media stuff:
www.MisterArt.com
www.DickBlick.com

The "Can't Live Without It" and "Gotta Have It" tools were especially
produced for me 'cuz I really wanted them, by one of the best places
to find anything and everything to do with sculpting! Check out their
selections of tools, and more:
www.sculpt.com (The Compleat Sculptor, New York)
phone: 800-9-SCULPT

Feathers are available at craft stores, but here's a nifty place to find
the more unusual stuff:
www.TheFeatherPlace.com (New York), phone: (212) 921-4452

Ammonites and other fossils can be found in places that specialize
in cut stones, minerals, and fossils. Look for the small ones that have
been cut and polished.

For fur, wool, and other natural products, try places that supply to
doll makers. Of course you can use real or synthetic yarns, too—
check out any fabric or yarn store for lots of choices. Make sure to
oven-test first.

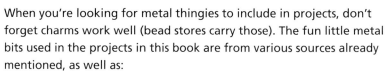

When you're looking for metal thingies to include in projects, don't forget charms work well (bead stores carry those). The fun little metal bits used in the projects in this book are from various sources already mentioned, as well as:

www.Metalliferous.com (New York), phone: (888) 944-0909

www.ThomasMann.com (Louisiana)

For more information on Paverpol and what to do with that fun product, visit their site: www.Paverpol.com.

GLASS BEAD ARTISTS

There are so many wonderful glass bead artists that I can't even begin to list them without missing some of my favorites. But, here are the ones whose beads I used in these projects:

Cheryl Harris created the flat glass beads that were the centers of the Funky Flowers: www.Cheryls-Art.net

Robin Foster's beads are in the Tidepool bowl and in the Funky Flowers projects (the knobby round ones): www.FosterFireGlass.com

I've used some of Jennifer Ringer's beads in some of the other pieces: www.SirensSongDesigns.net

I didn't use Nanette Young-Greiner's delicious beads in the Funky Flowers project, but they were the inspiration for them! www.ScorpioBeads.com

And, of course, those wonderful, wonderful glass eyeballs are made by artist Ralph McCaskey. You can get them on his site, www.NightSideStudios.com, and on my site.

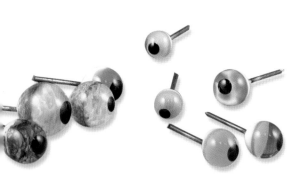

Information, discussion, and community

Here are the websites of most of the major polymer clay makers, for any additional information about their clays you may want:
www.Sculpey.com
www.Fimo.com
www.KatoPolyClay.com

The Internet is a wealth of information, discussion, and community for anyone who enjoys polymer clay and mixed media creating! Blogs, sites, groups—just search "polymer clay" and see where it leads you!

One of the best blogs to start your day in a polymer clay way is:
www.PolymerClayDaily.com

Other polymer clay must-visit sites are:
www.PolymerClayCentral.com
www.PolymerClayProductions.com

There are also several polymer clay chat groups, and Yahoo! groups. May I suggest joining mine? (Just type "CF originals" in the "Groups" section of www.Yahoo.com.)

Last but not least, the National Polymer Clay Guild is the place to go if you want to be part of the polymer clay community or just see what's going on. Visit the guild's site at: www.npcg.org. There are local guilds all over the country!

I don't want to make it seem like the United States has the corner on the market when it comes to polymer clay—sites, blogs, and groups abound internationally as well. Many of the above listed sites and blogs will link you to the global polymer clay community.

ADDITIONAL INFORMATION, BOOKS, PROJECTS, AND WORKSHOPS

There are also many wonderful books on polymer clay techniques and projects! Definitely peruse the craft section of your local or online bookstore for a wide selection.

For more information about using transfers with polymer clay, there are oodles of articles, videos, and chat group entries. The simplest way to find them is to search "polymer clay, transfers" and begin your journey of discovery!

And for another shameless bit of self-promotion, I have a series of smaller, how-to books on polymer clay. Visit my site for more information on the "Beyond Projects" series! www.CForiginals.com

A wonderful place to find lots of books on polymer clay and back issues of magazines with articles of interest to polymer clay enthusiasts is: www.PolkaDotCreations.com.

The magazine for polymer clay artists and enthusiasts is *PolymerCafé*. Find it in the magazine section of your bookstore, or online at: www.ScottPublications.com.

Need more projects? (Like, perhaps, that Green Guardian sculpture on page 142 of the Gallery or the fish in the Little Water World on page 94) I have a fun selection of projects available online:
www.CForiginals.com
or contact me :
Christi Friesen
PO Box 944
Tehachapi, CA 93581

About the Author

Christi Friesen was born at a very young age, kidnapped, and raised by lemmings. She escaped to California, where she got married, had various wonderful kids, and amassed credit card bills. She is currently considering having a midlife crisis, unless there's something good on television.

CF is an award-winning artist and her work has been featured in magazine articles, books, galleries, exhibits, and juried shows.

Index